Bitter Like A Lemon and the Abbey Theatre
in association with Dublin Port Company present

# IN OUR VEINS

by Lee Coffey

## ‖SAMUEL FRENCH‖

samuelfrench.co.uk

# THINKING ABOUT PERFORMING A SHOW?

**There are thousands of plays and musicals available to perform from Samuel French right now, and applying for a licence is easier and more affordable than you might think**

From classic plays to brand new musicals, from monologues to epic dramas, there are shows for everyone.

Plays and musicals are protected by copyright law, so if you want to perform them, the first thing you'll need is a licence. This simple process helps support the playwright by ensuring they get paid for their work and means that you'll have the documents you need to stage the show in public.

Not all our shows are available to perform all the time, so it's important to check and apply for a licence before you start rehearsals or commit to doing the show.

## LEARN MORE & FIND THOUSANDS OF SHOWS

Browse our full range of plays and musicals, and find out more about how to license a show
**www.samuelfrench.co.uk/perform**

Talk to the friendly experts in our Licensing team for advice on choosing a show and help with licensing
**plays@samuelfrench.co.uk    020 7387 9373**

# *Acting* Editions

## BORN TO PERFORM

**Playscripts designed from the ground up to work the way you do in rehearsal, performance and study**

---

*Larger*, clearer text for easier reading

*Wider* margins for notes

*Performance features* such as character and props lists, sound and lighting cues, and more

---

## + CHOOSE A SIZE AND STYLE TO SUIT YOU

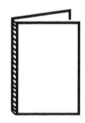

### STANDARD EDITION

Our regular paperback book at our regular size

### SPIRAL-BOUND EDITION

The same size as the Standard Edition, but with a sturdy, easy-to-fold, easy-to-hold spiral-bound spine

### LARGE EDITION

A4 size and spiral bound, with larger text and a blank page for notes opposite every page of text – perfect for technical and directing use

---

LEARN MORE | **samuelfrench.co.uk/actingeditions**

## MUSIC USE NOTE

Licensees are solely responsible for obtaining formal written permission from copyright owners to use copyrighted music in the performance of this play and are strongly cautioned to do so. If no such permission is obtained by the licensee, then the licensee must use only original music that the licensee owns and controls. Licensees are solely responsible and liable for all music clearances and shall indemnify the copyright owners of the play(s) and their licensing agent, Samuel French, against any costs, expenses, losses and liabilities arising from the use of music by licensees. Please contact the appropriate music licensing authority in your territory for the rights to any incidental music.

## USE OF COPYRIGHT MUSIC

A licence issued by Samuel French Ltd to perform this play does not include permission to use the incidental music specified in this copy.

Where the place of performance is already licensed by the PERFORMING RIGHT SOCIETY (PRS) a return of the music used must be made to them. If the place of performance is not so licensed then application should be made to the PRS, 2 Pancras Square, London, N1C 4AG.

A separate and additional licence from PHONOGRAPHIC PERFORMANCE LTD, 1 Upper James Street, London W1F 9DE (www.ppluk.com) is needed whenever commercial recordings are used.

## IMPORTANT BILLING AND CREDIT REQUIREMENTS

If you have obtained performance rights to this title, please refer to your licensing agreement for important billing and credit requirements.

## ABBEY THEATRE
### AMHARCLANN NA MAINISTREACH

**Abbey Theatre | Amharclann na Mainistreach**

The Abbey Theatre is Ireland's National Theatre. It was founded by W.B. Yeats and Lady Augusta Gregory. Since it first opened its doors in 1904 the theatre has played a vital and often controversial role in the artistic, social and cultural life of Ireland.

Inspired by the revolutionary ideals of its founders and its rich canon of Irish dramatic writing, the Abbey Theatre's mission is to imaginatively engage with all of Irish society through the production of ambitious, courageous and new theatre in all its forms. The Abbey Theatre commits to lead in the telling of the whole Irish story, in English and in Irish, and affirms that it is a theatre for the entire island of Ireland and for all its people. In every endeavour, the Abbey Theatre promotes inclusiveness, diversity and equality.

Over the years, the Abbey Theatre has premiered the work of major Irish playwrights such as J.M. Synge, Sean O'Casey and Teresa Deevy, as well as contemporary classics from Sebastian Barry, Dermot Bolger, Marina Carr, Shaun Dunne, Brian Friel, Thomas Kilroy, Frank McGuinness, Tom Murphy and Mark O'Rowe. In recent years, Irish and international audiences have enjoyed the plays of a new generation of playwrights, including Stacey Gregg, Nancy Harris, David Ireland, Deirdre Kinahan, Jimmy McAleavey, Owen McCafferty, Phillip McMahon, Elaine Murphy, Margaret Perry, Michael West and Carmel Winters.

In 1905 the Abbey Theatre first toured internationally and continues to be an ambassador for Irish arts and culture worldwide.

The Abbey Theatre gratefully acknowledges the support of the Arts Council.

Port Perspectives is Dublin Port Company's series of commissioned original artworks, installations and creative performances aimed at strengthening the bond between Dublin Port and the City.

Port Perspectives began with an open call to visual artists which resulted in three project commissions for a series of site-specific public artworks. Each of these commissions responded specifically to the built environment, local areas, history and context of Dublin Port. New works unveiled in 2017 included Sheelagh Broderick's *Port Walks*, Silvia Loeffler's *Transit Gateway*, and AEMI & Cliona Harmey's *port | river | city*.

These commissions were part of a larger programme of activity throughout 2017 which included Eugeen Van Mieghem: Port Life, a new exhibition sponsored by Dublin Port Company, which showed at Dublin City Gallery The Hugh Lane. The exhibition was supported by a programme of seminars and educational and outreach initiatives. Port Perspectives also included an arts engagement programme curated by Declan McGonagle and featured the sponsorship of Jesse Jones' Tremble Tremble, which represented Ireland at the 57th International Venice Biennale.

In 2019, Port Perspectives will involve a year of new Irish theatre commissions, featuring *In Our Veins* by Lee Coffey, a co-production between Bitter Like A Lemon and the Abbey Theatre, *What Lies Beneath – Port Stories* by The Lir Academy and Ringsend College, and an Abbey production, *Last Orders at the Dockside* by Dermot Bolger.

Port Perspectives builds on previous arts commissions by Dublin Port Company, including *Starboard Home* with the National Concert Hall – a new song cycle of Irish music and spoken word inspired by Dublin Port, Dublin City and the River Liffey; Cliona Harmey's Dublin Ships installation on the Scherzer Bridges in conjunction with Dublin City Council and the re-imagining of The Diving Bell on Sir John Rogerson's Quay.

## COMHLACHT CHALAFORT ÁTHA CLIATH
## DUBLIN PORT COMPANY

## LIFFEY WATER RUNS IN HIS VEINS

*In Our Veins* is the title of a new play from Bitter Like A Lemon Theatre Company, commissioned by Dublin Port Company as part of its Year of Theatre. Bitter Like A Lemon are a relatively new theatre company, having staged their first production in 2014, but Dublin Port Company CEO, Eamonn O'Reilly was suitably impressed by some of their previous productions to green-light *In Our Veins* in January 2018, when playwright Lee Coffey "went into full-on research mode".

Lee reached out to the Dublin Dockworkers Preservation Society, and pays huge tribute to the man who runs it, Declan Byrne, for putting him in touch with a host of retired dock workers.

"They had a lot of info about the area around the Monto, the North Inner City and what it was like at the time these men lived there, because obviously it's now completely different. A lot of things have been knocked down and the docks have totally changed."

Lee also took some inspiration from Dublin Port Company's Starboard Home project, where a host of Irish musicians penned songs based around the theme of the port, river and docklands. He spoke to some of the musicians involved about what influenced them in the creation of their music: "Lisa O'Neill actually released a brilliant video for her song, 'Rock The Machine', where she filmed a lot of the men I spoke to from the Dublin Dockworkers Preservation Society."

The support of businesses like Dublin Port Company is hugely welcomed by all arts groups and theatre companies, but particularly for smaller entities like Bitter Like A Lemon, for whom it was their first time being commissioned to produce a play.

## ABOUT THE AUTHOR

Lee Coffey is a writer from Dublin.

His shows include: *Leper + Chip* in Theatre Upstairs, Project Arts Centre, The Edinburgh Fringe Festival (Nominated for the Broadway Baby 5 Star Award and the National Student Drama Award for best play); *Electric Picnic* at The Lyric Belfast, The Axis, Cork and a production by Inis Nua in Philadelphia, USA; *Peruvian Voodoo* in Theatre Upstairs, 24 Hour Plays in the Abbey Theatre; *Slice, the Thief* in Smock Alley and The Axis; *Murder of Crows* in Theatre Upstairs, Project Arts Centre, Garter Lane and the Lyric Belfast; *From All Sides* in The Dublin Fringe Festival and a radio play, *The Matron for Dead Air* in the Bram Stoker Festival.

Lee was a participant in Rough Magic Theatre Company's SEEDS programme 2016/2017, Irish Theatre Institute's Six in The Attic Programme 2018/2019 and The New Playwrights' Programme in The Lyric, Belfast 2018.

He is a founding member of Bitter Like A Lemon Theatre Company.

## AUTHOR'S NOTE

*In Our Veins* was a commission from Dublin Port Company as a part of their Port Perspectives Initiative. They approached myself, Amilia Stewart and our company Bitter Like A Lemon to make a show for their year of theatre. It is a love letter to Dublin, in every sense. Putting a lens up to a world that no longer exists and that will never exist again. With the help of The Dublin Dockworkers Preservation Society and The North Inner City Folklore Project's publications of Dublin's social history, I hoped to put a mirror up to now by taking you back to a forgotten world. A world of tough choices, hardship and survival where human kindness knew no bounds, as the dark and unforgiving world took everything. It's a piece close to my heart and something I have been very proud to be a part of and I hope I've done it justice. It's a funny, dark and poignant look at where Dublin came from. Out of the shit and into the world.

*Lee Coffey, April 2019*

*In Our Veins* was first performed at the Abbey Theatre, Dublin on 10 April 2019 with the following cast and creatives:

| | |
|---|---|
| Ian Lloyd Anderson | Will, Michael, Paul, Patrick (1955) Whacker, Voice of Bloody (1970) |
| Jack Mullarkey | Stephen, Patrick (1938), Man, Bill |
| Aisling O'Mara | Sharon, Mary (1922 + 1938) Lily, Esther (1955) |
| Amilia Stewart | Kim, Anne, Woman, Margo |
| Catherine Byrne | Esther (2019) May, Mary (1955) |
| Gerard Byrne | Francis, Lynch, Doctor, Pawn, Bloody, Patrick (1970) |

| | |
|---|---|
| Writer | Lee Coffey |
| Director | Maisie Lee |
| Movement Director | Paula O'Reilly |
| Set and Costume Design | Lisa Krugel |
| Set and Costume Assistant | Jack Rogers |
| Lighting Design | Eoin Byrne |
| Composer and Sound Design | Denis Clohessy |
| Stage Manager | Evie McGuinness |
| Production Manager | Conor Mullan |
| Producer | Bitter Like A Lemon |
| Photography | Ste Murray |

## CHARACTERS

| | |
|---|---|
| WILL, MICHAEL, PAUL, PATRICK (1955), WHACKER, VOICE OF BLOODY (1970) | Actor One |
| STEPHEN, PATRICK (1938), MAN, BILL | Actor Two |
| SHARON, MARY (1922 + 1938), LILY, ESTHER (1955) | Actor Three |
| KIM, ANNE, WOMAN, MARGO | Actor Four |
| ESTHER (2019), MAY, MARY (1955) | Actor Five |
| FRANCIS, LYNCH, DOCTOR, PAWN, BLOODY, PATRICK (1970) | Actor Six |

VOICE: *Is designated by the director and actor is assigned to each line as seen fit*

There are no directions or definitive items needed for the performance. It should be at the director and designer's discretion as to how much or how little is used.

*This script went to press during rehearsals and may differ from the text in performance.*

## ACKNOWLEDGEMENTS

Amilia Stewart, Ger McNaughton, TileStyle, Business To Arts, Dance Ireland, the Abbey Theatre, Irish Theatre Institute, Karl Shiels, Laura Honan, Jimmy Fay, Annie Ryan, Lynne Parker, The North Inner City Folklore Project, The Dublin Dockworkers Preservations Society, Aaron Monaghan, Theatre Upstairs, Dublin Port Company, Paul Stewart, APT Workplace Pensions and the staff of Lanigans Pub.

*For my mother and father, Catherine and Denis.*

*The stage is empty. We hear the wind blowing and music playing. It continues through the overlapping dialogue. This can be repeated, depending on the director's preference.*

**VOICE** Down the docks.

**VOICE** Up the Monto.

**VOICE** In the Tenements.

**VOICE** The rot of Dublin.

**VOICE** Rats in your bed.

**VOICE** Flies in the walls.

**VOICE** The unfortunate girls.

**VOICE** The unfortunate boys.

**VOICE** The unfortunate families.

**VOICE** No work today.

**VOICE** No food today.

**VOICE** No hope today.

**VOICE** The worst slums in Europe.

**VOICE** Collapsing on us.

**VOICE** Killing us.

**VOICE** That's where Dublin came from.

**VOICES** Out of the shit.

**VOICES** And into the world.

*The lights flash and the outline of a coffin appears on the ground.*

**KIM**  Heya, Granda.

**SHARON**  You don't say, "Heya..." to your dead Granda.

**KIM**  What do you say then?

**SHARON**  I don't know.

*Pause.*

Alright, Granda.

*Pause.*

**KIM**  Is he supposed to look like that?

**SHARON**  Show some respect.

**KIM**  How do you know I didn't mean that in a positive way?

**SHARON**  Well, did you?

**KIM**  No, he looks awful.

**SHARON**  He's dead.

**KIM**  Thought they put make-up and that on him.

**SHARON**  They did.

**KIM**  Doesn't look it.

**SHARON**  We all don't have as much time as you.

**KIM**  Fuck off.

**SHARON**  Language.

*Pause.*

Caking yourself with it.

**KIM**  We fucking get it.

*Lights change. They both bless themselves.*

**ESTHER**  Now we'll say a little prayer. You start one there, Stephen.

*Pause.*

**STEPHEN** I don't know any, Nan.

**ESTHER** Some bleedin' Catholic you are. God forgive me for cursin'.

**STEPHEN** Sorry, Nan.

**ESTHER** It's okay, chicken. I'll teach you a few.

**ESTHER** *blesses herself and mouths a prayer to herself. She finishes it with, "Amen."*

Amen.

**STEPHEN** Amen.

*Pause.*

**ESTHER** He looks lovely, doesn't he?

**STEPHEN** Eh, he does, Nan.

**ESTHER** He always looked well.

**STEPHEN** He did.

**ESTHER** Even in death.

**STEPHEN** Eh, yeah.

**ESTHER** The bastard.

**STEPHEN** Nan.

**ESTHER** God forgive me for cursin'. It's a compliment, son. You'll have to glue me together when I'm dead.

**STEPHEN** Jaysus.

**ESTHER** I'll be fallin' off the bone an' that.

**STEPHEN** You'll look beautiful when you're dead, Nan.

**ESTHER** Thanks, darling. You're so sweet.

*Lights change.* **FRANCIS** *stands in silence for a moment.*

**FRANCIS** I'm going to miss you, Dad.

**WILL**  I'm sorry, Mr Doyle.

**FRANCIS**  Will?

**WILL**  Yeah.

**FRANCIS**  How did you end up in here with me?

**WILL**  Walked into the wrong room.

**FRANCIS**  Okay.

**WILL**  Was looking for the jacks.

**FRANCIS**  That's fine, son.

**WILL**  I'm dying for a sh/

**FRANCIS**  Don't finish that sentence.

**WILL**  Sorry.

**FRANCIS**  Where's me daughter?

**WILL**  She's outside with the rest of them.

**FRANCIS**  Alright.

>    *Silence.*

**WILL**  Never know what to say in situations like this.

**FRANCIS**  Silence is good, William.

>    *Lights change. Everyone is now at the coffin together.*

**SHARON**  Why are you in here?

**WILL**  Looking for the jacks.

**STEPHEN**  Thought it smelled a little funky.

**FRANCIS**  Shut up, you lot.

**ESTHER**  It was a lovely turnout, son.

**KIM**  Busiest wake I've ever seen.

**ESTHER**  Noticed a load of people missin' too/

**FRANCIS**  Ma/

ESTHER Those feckers are off my Christmas card list. God forgive me for cursin'.

FRANCIS Ma, let's just enjoy this time with Da.

ESTHER Sorry, son.

*Pause.*

He looks so lovely. My Patrick.

FRANCIS He does.

ESTHER What's that on him?

WILL Looks like lipstick.

SHARON Kim!

KIM Sorry, Nan. I just added a little colour to him.

STEPHEN Jesus Christ.

ESTHER Language, you. You little Protestant.

STEPHEN Nan.

ESTHER Don't Nan me, you. You didn't even know a prayer. Francis, do you know that?

FRANCIS What, Ma?

ESTHER This little Brit didn't know a single prayer to say to his poor Granda, God rest his soul.

SHARON Disgraceful.

KIM Yeah.

STEPHEN You two don't have a clue either.

KIM We do.

SHARON Yeah.

WILL I know a few.

ESTHER Son, be quiet. You're a little blow-in.

SHARON Nan/

ESTHER  A prayer, girls. For your Granda, Patrick.

STEPHEN  Come on, girls.

ESTHER  Off you go.

SHARON  Go on, Kim.

*They all drop their heads in respect. Pause.*

KIM  Em... *(speaks the first 3 lines of Dionne Warwick's "I SAY A LITTLE PRAYER")**

STEPHEN  Jaysus.

ESTHER  Have some respect, you!

STEPHEN  But Nan.

ESTHER  Shut your hole. Makin' me curse in front of me poor dead husband. Continue, dear.

*Pause.*

KIM  I run for the bus, dear.

While riding/

ESTHER  Riding?

KIM  Yeah.

ESTHER  You dirty little/

FRANCIS  Ma, it's not their fault.

ESTHER  Little heathens you've raised.

SHARON  Nan, nobody goes to mass anymore.

WILL  It's true, Mrs Doyle.

STEPHEN  Yeah, It's fucking/

FRANCIS  If you swear in this room again, I swear to God.

---

* A licence to produce IN OUR VEINS does not include a performance licence for "I SAY A LITTLE PRAYER". For further information, please see Music Use Note on page v.

ESTHER  Francis. I'll handle this. Stephen, I'll put you on your arse if you swear in front of your grandfather again. Now, apologise.

STEPHEN  Sorry, Granda.

FRANCIS  A lot of people don't go to mass anymore. It's a different world, Ma.

ESTHER  Who are you telling? No respect.

KIM  It's our choice, Nan.

ESTHER  Choice, you kids today know nothing of choice.

SHARON  What are you on about?

ESTHER  Not going to mass. That's a choice? You have no idea what it's like to be faced with an actual choice. One that would shape the generations to follow.

STEPHEN  We just don't like mass, Nan.

ESTHER  I'm not talking about mass!

FRANCIS  It's okay, Ma. We're all just a little worked up.

ESTHER  I'm not worked up. You children have no idea how easy you have it.

FRANCIS  Times change, it's not how it was when you were younger.

ESTHER  Who're you telling? The tough choices that have shaped our family, defined our family, they're lost on the youth of today.

KIM  You losing it, Nan?

WILL  Bit harsh.

STEPHEN  No, I think she might be.

ESTHER  Your poor great-grandmother.

SHARON  Yep, she's lost it.

**ESTHER**  Lost it, you watch yourself. Looking at me like I've ten heads. Have you not told them, Francis?

**SHARON**  Told us what?

*Pause.*

**FRANCIS**  No, I haven't, Ma.

**ESTHER**  Your grandfather there was given up! His poor mother, a lady of the Monto. Now there's a choice! Something you lot know nothing about.

**STEPHEN**  A prostitute?

**WILL**  Nice.

**ESTHER**  Although they were never called that in the day. Unfortunate girls is what they were called. Your Granda Patrick there was a Monto baby.

**STEPHEN**  What?

**FRANCIS**  He was born to one of the girls of the Monto.

**SHARON**  The Monto Monto.

**STEPHEN**  Like, "Take her up to Monto, Monto, Monto."

**KIM**  That Monto?

**WILL**  Great tune, that.

**FRANCIS**  Yes, that Monto.

**ESTHER**  Poor little Monto babies.

**KIM**  Jaysus.

**ESTHER**  Imagine that, giving up your child.

**SHARON**  I wouldn't wish that on anyone.

**ESTHER**  Your grandfather, born in a house on...Railway Street... in...nineteen twenty...two. I think. Wasn't it, Francis?

**FRANCIS**  Yeah, Ma.

**ESTHER**  Given up and raised by Paul and Mary Doyle.

ESTHER  She was a lovely woman. Always looked well, you know? They took in my Paddy out of the kindness of their hearts.

FRANCIS  They raised him. Never met me Granda Doyle.

ESTHER  Neither did I. Heard nothing but great things.

FRANCIS  Heard he was a hard man, a docker his whole life.

WILL  My Granda was a docker.

FRANCIS  Quiet time, Will.

WILL  Okay.

ESTHER  Many of the Monto babies were taken in by families. It was how it was in those days.

SHARON  So our name isn't Doyle?

FRANCIS  Your name is Doyle. As my name is Francis Doyle.

ESTHER  Her name was Anne Brady. She was one of the poor unfortunate girls that had nothing else but their bodies to sell. Down the Monto.

*The lights drop on the coffin and the other characters.*
ESTHER *walks forward. As she speaks, we start to hear*
VOICES *from the Monto streets coming through.*

VOICE  Howya, love.

VOICE  How much?

ESTHER  Young girls at the hands of ruthless madams.

VOICE  That May Oblong is an old cow.

ESTHER  In debt so they could never leave.

VOICE  Get out there and get my money back.

ESTHER  Surrounded by the poor.

VOICE  I own you.

ESTHER  And their children.

VOICE  Not in front of the kids.

ESTHER  No idea what was going on.

VOICE  Come on up the lane, love.

ESTHER  Oblivious and blissful in a rotten world.

    ESTHER *leaves.* ANNE *steps forward.*

VOICE  My girls are clean.

ANNE  I arrived in Dublin alone.

VOICE  The doctor has checked them all.

ANNE  To work.

VOICE  The prettiest girls in all of Dublin.

ANNE  But not like this.

VOICE  I'll take her.

VOICE  Those poor unfortunate girls.

    *Lights change to* ANNE BRADY, *1922.*

ANNE  Hello, I'm looking for a job.

VOICE  There's no work here.

ANNE  I was looking for any job.

VOICE  You were here yesterday.

ANNE  I was.

VOICE  We have nothin'.

ANNE  Nobody would take me. I was renting a room for a few
    shillings on Dominick Street. And no work was to be found.

VOICE  What do I look like?

ANNE  Please, I just need to find a job.

VOICE  Get out!

ANNE  I can get your rent. Please, I've nowhere to go.

**VOICE**  Not my problem.

**ANNE**  Please.

*Pause.*

In Dublin a few weeks and I'm out on the streets. Thought about going home but...but there was nothing there for me. Nothing here for me. Streets and streets of the poor. The poor helping the poor. Tenements over took Dublin and the hunger was overtaking me. I would get handouts from the Bayno or some bread from the kind tenants. Sleeping in their halls. Not a safe place to be. I'd lie in the darkest hall I could find. Unseen, a shadow to all that passed. Slept in the halls for many a night, on Railway Street. I found kind people here. Mary Doyle used to help me out each morning, a bit of bread here and there. She didn't have to 'cause I knew she had nothing.

**MARY** *is unseen.*

**MARY**  Take it.

**ANNE**  I can't.

**MARY**  Just take it, you're makin' a show of me.

**ANNE**  Wouldn't take no for an answer. She helped me many a morning. 'Til one day, I woke in the halls to a figure standing over me.

**MAY**  Howya, darling.

**ANNE**  Hello.

**MAY**  What's a pretty country girl like yourself doing sleeping rough?

**ANNE**  Just a little down on my luck is all.

**MAY**  A few people mentioned a pretty little thing sleeping in the halls.

**ANNE**  Who?

MAY  Some little birdies.

ANNE  I'll be fine.

MAY  Looking for work. Are we, love?

ANNE  I am.

MAY  And a place to stay?

ANNE  Yes.

MAY  I can help you with those things.

ANNE  Why?

MAY  It's what I do.

ANNE  It's what you do?

MAY  What's your name?

ANNE  Anne.

MAY  Nice to meet you, Anne. I'm May.

ANNE  May Oblong/

MAY  One and the same. How would you like to come work for me?

*Pause.*

It's getting cold out, love. You going to die in the hallways of the Monto? Or do you want to do something about it?

*Pause.*

Come on. A beautiful girl like yourself. There's nothing you can't get. If you really want it.

ANNE  Sleeping in the Monto, you hear names being said around the place.

VOICE  Cut-throats, those madams.

VOICE  Becky Cooper/

VOICE  Polly Butler/

VOICE  May Oblong/

ANNE  Dressed in the finest of clothes. A beautiful woman. Older now but you could still see it.

MAY  I can give you everything you need, girl. Fine clothes, money, a place to live.

ANNE  In return I'd...become one of her girls.

MAY  I'll look after you.

ANNE  It's not exactly something you want to be but/

MAY  I can hear the hunger crying from your stomach, love.

ANNE  And she was right.

MAY  Come work for me.

ANNE  I was going to starve to death.

MAY  I'll treat you well.

ANNE  If I didn't do something.

MAY  I can help you.

ANNE  And I let her.

MAY  That a girl. Listen to me and everything will be fine.

VOICE  New girl, May.

MAY  Shut your mouth, you.

VOICE  Another one falls into the trap.

MAY  Let's get you cleaned up, girl.

VOICE  Poor thing hasn't a clue.

ANNE  I rented a room from May. Like a lot of her girls did and we paid her out of the money we'd make. Off the streets and she fed and put new clothes on my back.

MAY  You look beautiful, love.

ANNE  She didn't give you the finest clothes to go standing on the street. Some girls were out there, on the corners, but she didn't put me there.

MAY  Anne, this is Lily.

LILY  Howya, love.

ANNE  Nice to meet you.

MAY  You're going with Lily.

ANNE  Where?

MAY  Grafton Street.

ANNE  For what?

LILY  I'll show you, love. Don't worry.

MAY  Mr Lynch is outside. Do me proud, girls.

ANNE  Mr Lynch worked for May. Bully boys they were called.
     Security for May's kip houses. If anyone got out of hand.
     Mr Lynch would see them out, with a few smacks for their
     troubles.

LYNCH  Let's go tempt the rich, girls.

LILY  May thinks highly o'you.

ANNE  What?

LILY  I mean, I don't blame her. A pretty little thing like yourself.

ANNE  Thanks, I suppose.

LILY  Over to Grafton Street and working from the flash houses.

ANNE  Is that not normal?

LILY  For the pretty ones it is. Keep the best for the rich, what?

ANNE  Lily worked in the flash houses. They're the best of the kip
     houses. The best girls for the wealthier clientele. May liked
     to show us off and today was my first taste of that. On the
     horse and trap over to Grafton Street. May liked to parade
     the girls to the rich. Lure them back with the best she had.

MAY  The young and the pretty.

LILY  Be nice, engage in conversation and the men will come
     visit later, love.

**ANNE**  Does this work?

**LILY**  May knows how to bait a hook, girl. Look at me, I'm fuckin' gorgeous.

**ANNE**  This was my first taste. Naive to it all.

**LILY**  Stop here, Lynchy.

**LYNCH**  Done, Lily.

**ANNE**  Lily always went to Grafton Street.

**LILY**  Hello, sir.

**ANNE**  And you could see why.

**LILY**  How are you today, love?

**ANNE**  She had a way with words.

**LILY**  You're a bit of a looker, aren't ya'?

**ANNE**  The men were drawn to her like a moth to a flame.

**LILY**  Look alive, yeah?

**ANNE**  Sorry, Lily.

**LILY**  The job's simple. Flirt and entice.

**ANNE**  Hello, sir!

**MICHAEL**  Jaysus, you know how to grab someone's attention.

**ANNE**  Sorry, didn't mean to startle you.

**MICHAEL**  It's okay. I'm Michael.

**ANNE**  Anne.

**MICHAEL**  How are you today, Anne?

**ANNE**  I'm good, thank you.

**MICHAEL**  Haven't seen you around before.

**ANNE**  I just came to Dublin.

**MICHAEL**  Thought the accent didn't fit.

ANNE  Yeah.

MICHAEL  How're you finding the big city?

ANNE  It has its adjustments.

MICHAEL  I'd say so, Dublin can be a scary place.

ANNE  It can but I think I'll get there.

MICHAEL  Course you will.

ANNE  He was nice, didn't go on like the rest.

MICHAEL  What part of the country you from then?

ANNE  Asked questions.

MICHAEL  Do you like it?

ANNE  About me.

MICHAEL  Do you miss home?

ANNE  As a person. It was nice.

LILY  Hey! Come here.

ANNE  What?

MICHAEL  Was great talking to you, Anne.

LILY  What are you doin'?

ANNE  What I'm supposed to be doing.

LILY  No, that isn't what we do. That was something else.

ANNE  I was talking.

LILY  Exactly, keep it professional.

ANNE  Okay, Lily.

LILY  It's what I'm here for.

ANNE  Once I got used to it, I was a natural. Mr Lynch would
park us up and men would walk over and say hello.

LILY  They're well aware of what we are and where we're from,
girl. So use that.

ANNE  But I always kept an eye for Michael.

LILY  Anne!

ANNE  And I think Lily knew.

LILY  Pay attention. Hello, sir.

ANNE  Pleasure to meet you.

VOICE  The pleasure's all mine.

ANNE  They would talk and ask what house we came from.

LILY  O'course/

ANNE  I'd love to take care of you/

LILY  I'll play nice/

ANNE  Unless you don't want me to/

LILY  You know where to find me/

ANNE  I'll be waiting for you/

LILY  I look forward to seeing you/

ANNE  Soon, I hope.

VOICE  Very soon.

ANNE  Goodbye, sir.

LILY  Pleasure to meet you.

ANNE  No sign today either.

LILY  Let's get movin', Lynchy.

LYNCH  No bother, Lily.

ANNE  When we got back, May would be there waiting for us.
     Every time.

MAY  How did it go, girls? Catch any?

LILY  We were busy today, May.

MAY  We better be.

ANNE  You wouldn't know if it was a success until a few days later. If the men came wandering into the house and asked for you. My first time with someone was/

VOICE  I don't want to talk.

ANNE  Okay.

VOICE  Get on the bed.

ANNE  I did.

VOICE  Take your clothes off.

ANNE  I did.

VOICE  Now open your legs.

ANNE  And like that I was one of May's girls. I had to turn my head so he wouldn't see the tears rolling down my face.

VOICE  Yeah, turn away.

ANNE  He finished and got off me.

VOICE  I enjoyed you, darling. Be seeing you again.

*Pause.*

ANNE  I stood naked and looked at myself in the mirror.

*Pause.*

That was the last time I ever cried.

LILY  The first time is always tough.

ANNE  That was my first time, Lily.

LILY  I know, girl.

ANNE  My first time ever.

LILY  Ah, girl. I'm so sorry.

ANNE  There was blood on the bed.

LILY  You just had to get through it, girl.

ANNE  I felt worthless, dirty/

LILY  It gets easier/

ANNE  I just want to wash him off me.

LILY  It'll pass.

ANNE  And it did.

LILY  You become numb.

ANNE  And feel nothing.

LILY  And get on with it.

ANNE  I wasn't going to starve on the streets.

LILY  Exactly.

ANNE  It's survival/

LILY  You do what you must to stay alive.

ANNE  You have to.

LILY  Now, come on, we get you a drink.

ANNE  I became great friends with Lily, looked out for each other. She'd do anything for you. She'd see the little kids on the street with things under their arm/

LILY  Where are you off to with that parcel?

VOICE  I am going to the pawn with my granny's shawl.

LILY  How much are you asking on it?

VOICE  Five shillings.

ANNE  Lily would turn to the other girls, including myself and we'd all chip in for the kid.

LILY  Take that and go home to your granny, give her back her shawl and give her that money. You don't be coming down this lane to go to the pawn again. Or I'll batter ya'.

ANNE  You'd always see the kids getting money off her.

LILY  What did I tell you?

VOICE  Not to be going to the pawn.

**LILY**  They're your daddy's boots.

**VOICE**  He told me to go. What d'ya want me to do, Lily? Jaaaaysus.

**LILY**  Enough o'that lip.

**ANNE**  Another whip around.

**LILY**  Take this home. Your daddy might need them boots if he gets a job.

**ANNE**  This happened again and again. She'd send the children on jobs too.

**LILY**  Over to the ballast office with ya', beside O'Connell Bridge.

**ANNE**  She'd have them ask what time such a ship was coming into Dublin.

**LILY**  If the man asks why, tell him your daddy works on the ship.

**VOICE**  But he doesn't.

**LILY**  He doesn't need to know that.

**ANNE**  They'd come back and she'd give them a shilling.

**LILY**  Now get out of here, you. Go home with that money.

**VOICE**  Thanks, Lily.

**ANNE**  Ships coming in meant there were men coming in.

**LILY**  Hundreds of them and as horny as the day is long.

**ANNE**  And she was right. My time with May went quick. Before I knew where I was I was one of her main girls.

**MAY**  You're one of my best, Anne.

**ANNE**  Thanks for helping me, May.

**MAY**  I help you, you help me. That's how this works.

**ANNE**  One day May was sending us over to Grafton Street again.

**MAY**  You're taking Julia.

ANNE  Where's Lily?

MAY  I've another job for Lily.

ANNE  But she usually/

MAY  I've another job for Lily.

ANNE  Lynchy picked up myself and Julia. A nice girl. Around
a couple of months. All of a sudden I was Lily. Taking the
lead and showing her the ropes. On the way I told her what
to do and she was a natural.

MICHAEL  Good afternoon.

ANNE  Well hello, stranger.

MICHAEL  Fine day, isn't it?

ANNE  You didn't come over to talk about the weather now.

MICHAEL  What if I did?

ANNE  You didn't.

MICHAEL  I didn't, no. How have you been?

ANNE  Okay, yourself?

MICHAEL  I've been grand, thanks.

ANNE  Glad to hear it.

MICHAEL  Over here a lot these days?

ANNE  A bit, haven't seen you around.

MICHAEL  All the men pestering you.

ANNE  Ah no, it is what it is.

MICHAEL  Do you like any of these men then?

ANNE  The odd one is alright looking.

MICHAEL  Oh yeah?

ANNE  Yeah. Some are very attractive.

MICHAEL  Yeah?

ANNE  Not you though.

MICHAEL  What?

ANNE  Ah you're a bit mad looking.

MICHAEL  I'm not mad looking.

ANNE  Ah you are. Look at you. Big head on ya'.

MICHAEL  Here, my head is a normal size for a man my height.

ANNE  The doctors tell you that?

MICHAEL  They fucking did actually.

ANNE  Swearing an' all now. You didn't like that comment, did you?

MICHAEL  Little sensitive about it, that's all.

ANNE  And nothing wrong with that.

MICHAEL  Nothing wrong with that at all.

ANNE  A sensitive man can be a good thing.

MICHAEL  It can.

ANNE  But it doesn't suit you.

MICHAEL  Thanks, bleedin' delighted I came over.

ANNE  Me too.

MICHAEL  Oh yeah?

ANNE  Nah, will you piss off?

MICHAEL  Ah for fuck/

ANNE  I'm messing. I am glad you came over.

MICHAEL  Seriously?

ANNE  I am, do be looking out for you.

MICHAEL  I do keep an eye for you myself when I'm around here.

ANNE  That's nice to hear.

**LYNCH**  Time to go, girls.

**ANNE**  Shite, I've to go. See you soon?

**MICHAEL**  I'd like that.

**ANNE**  As we pull off, Michael stood and watched us down Grafton Street. I couldn't help but think of his life. What he did, where he went, where he lived. What a fine thing it would be to be away from this and with a man like that.

**LYNCH**  What's going on?

**ANNE**  We got close to home and there was commotion in the air.

**LYNCH**  What the fuck is going on?

**ANNE**  People running towards Corporation Street.

**VOICE**  They're batterin' each other.

**ANNE**  Who is?

**VOICE**  Tearin' out of each other they are.

**ANNE**  We get closer and there's a crowd in the middle of the street.

**VOICE**  Bait her, Lily!

**ANNE**  Lily?

**LYNCH**  Where you going?

**ANNE**  I jumped down. Pushed my way through the crowds and I see Lily and May tearing out of each other.

**VOICE**  She deserves it, Lily.

**VOICE**  She's an old cow.

**ANNE**  What happened?

**MAY**  Steal from me, you little bitch.

**ANNE**  Is that true, Lily?

**LILY**  I told you, I didn't fuckin' take anything.

MAY  I know you did. You were in my shop, there's money missing from the register and my gold brooch is gone! My solid-gold brooch!

LILY  I'd look elsewhere because it wasn't me.

MAY  Admit it before/

LILY  Before you get one of your dodgy coppers down.

MAY  If you think you can sell that brooch in this city, you're a fool. I'll notify every dealer in town.

LILY  I didn't take your tacky little brooch, May.

MAY  You're gone.

LILY  Good. Don't need you anyway, you fat aul' cow.

ANNE  Don't do this, May. Please.

LILY  Leave it, Anne. I'll be grand.

ANNE  Lily, you can't/

LILY  I'll be okay, girl.

LYNCH  Let's get you inside, May.

MAY  Come on, Anne.

> *Pause.*

> Anne!

ANNE  What?

MAY  Now.

ANNE  I look at Lily.

LILY  Go. I'll be fine. You can't afford to join me.

ANNE  Lily smiles at me. Then I slowly follow May into the house.

LILY  Stay strong, girl.

ANNE  I walk through the door and it closes behind me.

MAY  You little bitch.

**ANNE**  May smacks me across the face.

**MAY**  Bitch.

**ANNE**  Again.

**MAY**  Bitch.

**ANNE**  Again.

**MAY**  Bitch!

**ANNE**  Again.

*Pause.*

**MAY**  The next time you disobey me like that in front of people, you're out on your arse.

**ANNE**  May/

**MAY**  There'll be no more discussion on the matter. Now go wash yourself and get to work.

**ANNE**  That was the first time I saw that side to May. She was like a coin. A saint on one side and the devil on the other. She gave to charity, looked after the poor but she had this streak. She'd turn and put the fear of God in you. From that day on, I kept her at a distance. Lily kept working. She became known as Lily of the Lamp Post. She stood every night outside Jack Maher's pub under the lamp post. The light shining on her beautiful face. I missed her. May didn't want me near her and I wasn't getting the smacks again. I'd see her a little during the day but once the sun went down, I went back to the flash house. And tonight started just like any other. Until a face I knew came strolling by.

**MICHAEL**  Hello again, Anne.

**ANNE**  It was Michael. Here, to see me.

**MICHAEL**  How've you been?

**ANNE**  I'm good, I'm surprised to see you here.

**MICHAEL**  I wanted to see you.

ANNE  You did?

MICHAEL  Yeah.

ANNE  Why don't we go upstairs?

MICHAEL  Okay.

ANNE  We go into a room. Are you okay?

MICHAEL  Yeah, just never been to a place like this before.

ANNE  They have their moments.

MICHAEL  The prices are extortion.

ANNE  You can't just walk into May's place.

MICHAEL  Yeah, you've to pay.

ANNE  She says you have to pay for what's good in this world.

MICHAEL  I've never done anything like this before.

ANNE  It's okay, don't worry. I'll look after you.

MICHAEL  I just wanted to see you.

ANNE  He's come to see me.

MICHAEL  I can't stop thinking about you.

ANNE  Maybe he can stop all this.

MICHAEL  I had to come here/

ANNE  I can leave here/

ANNE/MICHAEL  Today/

MICHAEL  With you.

ANNE  With him.

MICHAEL  Sit on the bed.

ANNE  On the bed?

MICHAEL  Yes.

ANNE  He walks over.

MICHAEL  Anne.

ANNE  Sits beside me.

MICHAEL  I had to come here.

ANNE  He looks at me.

MICHAEL  Had to.

ANNE  We kiss.

> *Pause.*

MICHAEL  Lie down.

ANNE  I do.

MICHAEL  Don't move.

ANNE  He grabs me.

MICHAEL  You teased me.

ANNE  He was so rough.

MICHAEL  Do what I say.

ANNE  Pinned me down.

MICHAEL  Stay there!

ANNE  So aggressive.

MICHAEL  Don't move.

ANNE  With an anger he never had.

MICHAEL  I said don't move.

ANNE  He was on top of me, looked right into my eyes. Kissed me again.

> *Pause.*

MICHAEL  I shouldn't have come here.

ANNE  And jumped off me.

MICHAEL  It was a sin to come here. This place is the devil's playground.

ANNE  Michael, it's okay.

MICHAEL  Don't touch me.

ANNE  I'm here, relax. It's okay.

MICHAEL  I need to go.

ANNE  Please, don't go. We can talk about this.

MICHAEL  There's nothing to talk about.

ANNE  I like you, Michael.

MICHAEL  You're nothing but a dirty tramp.

ANNE  You say that now/

MICHAEL  Tramp/

ANNE  When you're not on top of me.

MICHAEL  We did nothing!

ANNE  He pushes me to the ground.

MICHAEL  You're not getting one shilling from me.

ANNE  I don't want your money, Michael.

MICHAEL  Do you hear me?

ANNE  He punches me in the face.

MICHAEL  Not one shilling.

ANNE  And again.

MICHAEL  You're going to hell.

ANNE  And again.

MICHAEL  All of you. You're all going to hell.

ANNE  The door is pushed open and Lynchy reefs him off me.

LYNCH  You little bastard.

MICHAEL  Tramp!

LYNCH  Get the fuck out of here!

ANNE  Lynchy drags him down the hall. I can hear him and the other boys going at him. Baiting him. May came in a moment after.

MAY  The dirty bastard. You poor thing. What happened?

ANNE  I tell her.

MAY  Go home and get cleaned up. Take the rest of the night off.

ANNE  Two sides of a coin. The devil and the saint.

MAY  I'll check on you tomorrow.

ANNE  I liked May the saint. That night I sat in my room and looked out the window. I thought about Michael, and how I would never drop my guard again. Lily was right. I sat and watched the girls go down the man trap with man after man and then come legging it back out after they had robbed them.

VOICE  Me fuckin' money.

VOICE  I didn't take anythin'.

VOICE  Then why are you runnin'?

VOICE  Exercise is good for ya' an' all that.

ANNE  I saw girls fighting over clients, pulling the hair off each other.

VOICE  He was with me first.

VOICE  Me arse he was.

ANNE  And I saw Lily, as beautiful as ever, standing under her light. The Monto was a horrible place but it kept a lot of people alive, fed families and kept a roof over their heads. And among all the death, poverty and sex there was some beauty. And on the quiet nights, like tonight, voices would rise from the darkness and lift your heart. The girls, singing as they waited.

*The girls sing, a song full of sorrow and hardship.*

**VOICE**  Howya, love?

**VOICE**  Can we go somewhere?

**ANNE**  It was a special place, I think.

Soon after, my eyes healed and I was back to work as before. I went to see Lily but she hadn't been around.

**VOICE**  Haven't seen her.

**ANNE**  Strange.

**VOICE**  Not in ages.

**ANNE**  She was gone.

**VOICE**  Must have left.

**ANNE**  A few days later I woke up and I started to get sick. This happened over and over for a few weeks so I went to Jervis Street Hospital to see a doctor.

**DOCTOR**  What seems to be the problem?

**ANNE**  I haven't been feeling the best lately, doctor.

**DOCTOR**  Okay. Let me take a look.

**ANNE**  He asked me a couple of questions.

**DOCTOR**  Okay, Mrs Brady. I think you might be pregnant.

**ANNE**  Sorry.

**DOCTOR**  All the symptoms are there. Missed period, morning sickness/

**ANNE**  I can't be pregnant.

**DOCTOR**  I cannot confirm yet but we will see in a few weeks when you start to show.

*Pause.*

Congratulations, Mrs Brady.

ANNE  Thanks, doctor.

DOCTOR  See you in a couple of weeks.

ANNE  I left the hospital and walked. I'm pregnant. What the fuck am I going to do? I went about the next few weeks as normal and I knew. The doctor was right, I could feel it. I was tired, sore and didn't feel well at all. I didn't know what to do. I couldn't tell anyone. I went looking for Lily again but she really was gone.

MAY  You okay, Anne?

ANNE  I am. Why?

MAY  I don't know. You don't seem yourself.

ANNE  Just had a late night last night is all.

MAY  Okay then.

ANNE  May was a like a hawk. I had seen what she did to pregnant girls.

MAY  Get out of here.

VOICE  Please, May.

MAY  You're no use to me. You pregnant little bitch.

VOICE  I've nowhere to go.

MAY  Who'd pay for that?

ANNE  Gone. It happened many a time around the streets. Kicked out with nothing and nowhere to go. May kept most of your money so you had to keep working to keep living. Once you were pregnant, you were cut off, banished. And it was only a matter of time for me. A few months later May called a few of us into her shop.

MAY  Girls, I've some new dresses for you. Have to keep you in the best to attract the best.

ANNE  There were three of us in there.

MAY  Let's get theses dresses tried on.

ANNE  The girls took them in the back and changed.

MAY  In you go, Anne.

ANNE  I followed. I was in trouble. I had been wearing baggie dresses and clients were too drunk to notice anything.

MAY  Come on out and let me see you, girls.

ANNE  The dress didn't fit me.

MAY  Gorgeous. Now you, Anne.

ANNE  I don't move.

MAY  Anne?

ANNE  She's banging on the door.

MAY  Don't have me ask again.

ANNE  I walk out. Dress in hand.

MAY  What's wrong?

ANNE  Before I can utter a word.

MAY  Get out!

ANNE  May, please.

MAY  How long have you been hiding this?

ANNE  I can keep working, May.

MAY  You're damaged. Who'd pay for that?

ANNE  Who'd pay for that? Exactly like I heard her say it to many others before me.

MAY  I never want to see you again.

ANNE  And she pushed me out the door of her shop and onto the street.

MAY  Get out of my sight, you and your little bastard.

ANNE  May/

MAY  Now/

ANNE  One last punch to the face from May Oblong and I fell on to the ground.

VOICE  Jaysus, May's at it again.

VOICE  Poor girl.

ANNE  I didn't even respond, I just walked away. To where? I had no idea.

VOICE  Get pregnant and you're gone.

VOICE  Not the first.

VOICE  Certainly not the last.

ANNE  I had a couple of shillings and that was it. I was back to where I started.

MAY  The room is mine, these clothes are mine, and any money you earned is mine!

ANNE  All I had was a couple of dresses and a life in my stomach. The first thing I did was walk to Jack Rafter's and pawn everything I had.

PAWN  This stuff is no use to me, girl.

ANNE  Please, I'm pregnant and I have nothing.

PAWN  I'll give you two shillings. It's not worth anything near that.

ANNE  Thank you.

PAWN  Just keep it between us, it's bad for business.

*Pause.*

ANNE  And I was back in the hallways as the Monto lived on around me.

VOICE  Come on, girls.

VOICE  How much, love?

VOICE  You dirty bastard, get the fuck out of here.

VOICE  Don't fucking touch me, you!

ANNE  I passed through the streets for those months, just staying alive. Some of the girls helped me and some of the families would too. Bread and tea in the morning or a smile as they passed me in the doorway. As Lily said, you do what you must to stay alive. And I did. I was a couple months pregnant and a voice woke me.

VOICE  Here, I know you. You worked for May, didn't you?

ANNE  I did.

VOICE  I always wanted a go o'you.

ANNE  Leave me alone.

VOICE  But couldn't afford ya'. How about now?

ANNE  Leave me alone.

VOICE  I've a couple of shillings.

ANNE  Please, leave me alone.

VOICE  Alright, don't blame me when you starve.

*Pause.*

VOICE  Your little baby too.

*Pause.*

ANNE  I'd love to tell you that I didn't...but I did. I had to. For the little baby to live, I had to. For me to live, I had to. When you can't go any lower time seems to blur. Moves at its own pace.

VOICE  Come on, girls.

VOICE  How much, love?

VOICE  You dirty bastard, get the fuck out of here.

VOICE  Don't fucking touch me, you!

ANNE  Days, weeks, months. They all seem to repeat.

VOICE  Come on, girls.

VOICE  How much, love?

VOICE  You dirty bastard, get the fuck out of here.

VOICE  Don't fucking touch me, you!

ANNE  Over and over until, fuck! The pain.

VOICE  You okay?

VOICE  Here, I'm not bleedin' able for this!

VOICE  Get help!

ANNE  Next you're in a tenement room giving birth. The pain. Two women.

Helping me. Telling me to push. And I did. In the blur of it all I saw Lily. She was beside me.

LILY  Push, girl.

ANNE  Lily?

LILY  I'm with you. Push.

ANNE  Where have you been?

LILY  It doesn't matter, I'm here now. Push.

ANNE  I push.

LILY  There you go.

ANNE  I give one last push and a baby's cry fills the dark room.

LILY  You did it. I'm so proud of you, girl.

ANNE  I close my eyes for a moment, open them and she's gone. Lily?

*Pause.*

Where's Lily? Did she leave?

MARY  There was nobody else here, darling.

ANNE  I look down at the baby. My baby. A beautiful little boy.
His little eyes lighting up the room.

MARY  He's so beautiful.

ANNE  He is. Too beautiful for me.

MARY  What will you call him?

ANNE  Patrick.

MARY  Suits him.

ANNE  Thank you. The doctor came and the women paid for
it out of their own pocket. Maureen Plunkett and Mary
Doyle. The lady that had helped me when I slept rough.
I rested for a day or two, it had been snowing and it was
bitter cold out. I gathered my strength and I left the house.
They said goodbye and I thanked them. It was night and
I had planned on staying with one of the girls on Foley
Street around the corner. As I left the house, there was a
lady lying in the doorway. She was wearing a dress that
I knew well. I stood over her and it was Lily. She was half
the woman she was. Her beautiful face sunken in on itself,
she was frozen solid. Lily?

*Pause.*

I looked at Lily and I looked at Patrick. I knew. If I kept him
it wasn't going to end well for him. He was too beautiful
for me and he needed to stay that way. The voices on the
streets played out once more.

VOICE  Come on, girls.

VOICE  How much, love?

VOICE  You dirty bastard, get the fuck out of here.

VOICE  Don't fucking touch me, you!

ANNE  And I turned and walked up the stairs. To the room
I had just left, Mary Doyle's room. I put my son on the
floor, knocked on the door and walked away. I went to the

floor below and heard the door opening. I heard Mary and her husband, Paul.

**MARY**  It's Patrick.

**PAUL**  What?

**MARY**  The girl we helped.

**PAUL**  Where's she?

**MARY**  Anne?

**ANNE**  I stay silent.

**MARY**  Anne, are you there?

**ANNE**  Silent.

**PAUL**  What do we do?

**MARY**  Let's get him inside.

**PAUL**  We've enough to be dealing with, Mary.

**MARY**  He'll die out there.

**ANNE**  And they closed their door.

*Pause.*

I lied when I said my first night with a man was the last time I ever cried. I couldn't stop. But that baby deserved better. They would give him a life and I would give him nothing but misery.

*Pause.*

I stepped outside into the snow and walked down Railway Street, Gardiner Street and down to the Liffey. I walked in the snow all night and I never went back to the Monto ever again. The years passed and I heard he was raised as a gentleman. Little Patrick. And started working with his Da, Paul, on the docks.

*As **ANNE** talks, we start to hear **VOICES** from the docks coming through.*

VOICE  Only one ship for Palgrave Murphy's.

VOICE  I won't get near that with his three or four gangs.

ANNE  I missed him.

VOICE  There are two ships up for George Bell.

ANNE  But my life wasn't for him.

VOICE  Paddy Nolan's, I might a get job there.

ANNE  Life on the streets isn't for a child.

VOICE  I wouldn't get a job there in Betson's.

ANNE  So I did what was best.

VOICE  How many ships are on the South Quay?

ANNE  It never leaves me.

VOICE  Right, I'll try over there.

ANNE  And haunted me for the rest of my days.

> ANNE *leaves.*

VOICE  Right, calm down.

PAUL  Follow me, son.

VOICE  Get out of me way!

PATRICK  Right, Da.

VOICE  Here, I was here first.

PAUL  Don't let them push you around.

VOICE  Me arse you were.

VOICE  Fuckin' was!

> *Lights change to* PAUL *and* PATRICK. *1938.*

PATRICK  That morning was my first time down the docks.

PAUL  Are you right?

PATRICK  First experience of the read.

PAUL  I'm goin'.

PATRICK  The first of many.

PAUL  Stay here then.

PATRICK  He had no patience. I caught up with him on the quays.

PAUL  You're lucky.

PATRICK  Freezin' and the sun isn't even up yet.

PAUL  Keep up.

PATRICK  This is miles away.

PAUL  It isn't.

PATRICK  It was.

PAUL  It's around the corner.

PATRICK  It wasn't.

PAUL  Maybe if you got up earlier.

PATRICK  Was fuckin' Baltic.

PAUL  Language, you little bollocks.

PATRICK  Freezin'.

PAUL  Move.

PATRICK  I am.

PAUL  It's seven.

PATRICK  So early.

PAUL  Shut up.

PATRICK  Why are they so early?

PAUL  Goin' to have them at fuckin' night, are they?

PATRICK  Just wrecked is all.

PAUL  Then go to bed earlier.

PATRICK  I was in bed at ten last night.

**PAUL** Clearly wasn't enough.

**PATRICK** The rats are doin' me head in.

**PAUL** You were raised with rats.

**PATRICK** They're getting louder.

**PAUL** They're not.

**PATRICK** They are.

**PAUL** Just movin'.

**PATRICK** Scurryin'.

**PAUL** As always.

**PATRICK** It's from Betty Nugent next door.

**PAUL** What?

**PATRICK** Betty was pregnant. Me Da didn't believe what they were after.

**PAUL** Bollocks.

**PATRICK** See.

**PAUL** That's how they've always been.

**PATRICK** She just had little Padraig.

**PAUL** That's what they're after?

**PATRICK** Yeah.

**PAUL** Bollocks.

**PATRICK** She's breast feedin'.

**PAUL** So?

**PATRICK** The rats are drawn out by the smell of her milk.

**PAUL** Jaysus.

**PATRICK** You can hear her and Mr Nugent screamin' in the night.

**VOICE** They're out again!

VOICE  Get! You filthy bastards!

VOICE  They're after the baby.

VOICE  Smelly fuckers, get!!!

PAUL  Enough of this.

PATRICK  I'm gettin' a dog, Da.

PAUL  A dog?

PATRICK  Yeah.

PAUL  No.

PATRICK  A Kerry blue.

PAUL  We're nearly there, come on.

PATRICK  I'm gettin' a dog.

PAUL  You're not.

PATRICK  There's a fella on Corporation Street that breeds and trains them.

PAUL  Fair play to him.

PATRICK  He gets a barrel, puts three fully grown rats in it then drops the pup in.

PAUL  Bollocks!

PATRICK  Truth! The rats attack the pup but the pup fights back, killin' the lot. The last time that pup is ever bitten by a rat. It teaches the pup to hate them. Killin' any it finds.

PAUL  Lovely story, son.

PATRICK  The poxy truth.

PAUL  If I agree, will you hurry?

PATRICK  I will.

PAUL  We'll get one.

PATRICK  Yes!

PAUL  Now fuckin' walk!

PATRICK  I did. Miles down the Liffey to Palgrave Murphy's.

PAUL  We're tryin' here for somethin' different, son. The bastard at Custom House has his own house gangs so we'll never get in.

PATRICK  We approach.

PAUL  It's quarter past seven, good time.

PATRICK  Hundreds of men.

PAUL  Follow me.

PATRICK  Around a platform.

PAUL  Stay close.

PATRICK  They talk but they're alert.

PAUL  We've a few minutes before we start.

PATRICK  The sun slowly risin' and lightin' the harbour.

PAUL  Your first read, son.

PATRICK  Couldn't have tried nearer the house?

PAUL  Lazy bastard.

PATRICK  Me Da filled me in.

PAUL  Thousands of men on Dublin's wharfs, Patrick.

PATRICK  Troops of them.

PAUL  All lookin' for work.

PATRICK  From local areas.

VOICE  Sheriff Street.

VOICE  Ringsend.

VOICE  Pearse Street.

PATRICK  They would gather at/

VOICE  Custom House Quay.

VOICE  North Wall Quay.

VOICE  City Quay.

PAUL  And many more.

PATRICK  The aim of all these men.

PAUL  To be chosen for work, son.

PATRICK  Me Da tried his hand at most.

PAUL  Some days you work.

PATRICK  Some days you don't.

PAUL  But down here, son.

PATRICK  Yeah?

PAUL  I'm slightly known here.

PATRICK  So we might have a shot.

PAUL  It's about being known, son.

PATRICK  A man walks up an' onto the platform.

PAUL  Here we go.

PATRICK  The crowd comes alive.

VOICE  Right, calm down.

PAUL  Follow me, son.

VOICE  Get out of me way!

PATRICK  Right, Da.

VOICE  Fuck you, I was here first.

PAUL  Don't let them push you around.

VOICE  Me arse you were.

VOICE  Fuckin' was!

PATRICK  The man steps forward.

PAUL  The stevedore, Patrick.

**PATRICK**  He's who you need to be seen by.

**PAUL**  Get in with him and you're in.

**PATRICK**  He starts to call out names.

**VOICE**  Are there any Nevins here?

**PATRICK**  A man steps forward.

**PAUL**  This is bollocks.

**PATRICK**  What's happening?

**PAUL**  He's callin' his house gangs.

**PATRICK**  Regular workers of his.

**PAUL**  Fuck.

**PATRICK**  Then the stevedore called out name after name.

**VOICE**  Murphy.

**VOICE**  Behan.

**VOICE**  Carrick.

**VOICE**  McDermott.

**PAUL**  Fuck's sake.

**PATRICK**  Name after name.

**PAUL**  Men he knew.

**PATRICK**  Before we knew what was happenin'/

**PAUL**  Fuck.

**PATRICK**  That was that. He called the men he wanted for work and the rest were left.

**PAUL**  Tough luck.

**PATRICK**  Try another day.

**PAUL**  Done.

**PATRICK**  What?

PAUL  Come on.

PATRICK  Where we goin'?

PAUL  Just follow me.

PATRICK  We walked, as did many a man, to Macken's pub, down near Spencer Dock.

PAUL  Two pints.

PATRICK  This was the first time me Da bought me a pint. Da?

PAUL  There you are.

PATRICK  We stood at the bar, an old timer sat at the end of it.

PAUL  Here. Your first.

PATRICK  I took a sup. Tasted like shite.

PAUL  You'll get used to it.

PATRICK  The old timer knew me Da.

BLOODY  Howya, Paulie.

PAUL  Alright, Bloody.

BLOODY  This the youngfella?

PATRICK  Howya/

PAUL  His first day on the docks.

BLOODY  It's goin' well then.

PATRICK  Read didn't go as we hoped.

BLOODY  You'll get used to it.

PAUL  Was down the point. No joy.

BLOODY  You'll never get in with that fella. His gangs come first.

PAUL  I know, I haven't had much luck elsewhere so/

BLOODY  Thought you'd give it a try.

PAUL  And here I am.

**PATRICK**   This can't be the only way to get work.

**PAUL**   It's how it is.

**PATRICK**   Standin' in the cold and hopin' to get called, that's it?

**BLOODY**   He catches on fast.

**PATRICK**   Surely you've been around long enough to be known?

**BLOODY**   You little/

**PAUL**   He has a point.

*Pause.*

**BLOODY**   True.

**PAUL**   What did you do?

**BLOODY**   Had a bit of a scrap last night.

**PAUL**   With who?

**BLOODY**   Micka Kelly.

**PAUL**   'Cause he didn't call you at the read?

**BLOODY**   He did call me at the read.

**PAUL**   Nice way o'showin' your thanks.

**BLOODY**   We were working on a timber ship yesterday. And after we headed to Butt Bar to get paid. And I hadn't been with these boys before. He paid me and I was half a crown short.

**PAUL**   For the stevedore/

**BLOODY**   Or the fucking bar man.

**PATRICK**   For what?

**PAUL**   The bar man takes a cut, son. For handlin' the money.

**BLOODY**   Most of your work will be paid out in a pub, lad.

**PAUL**   They've the change to pay all the boys.

**BLOODY**   And I said to the stevedore.

**PAUL**   He's the fella that employs you, son.

PATRICK  I know.

BLOODY  I said to him, "If I want to pay anyone, I'll do it meself."
So I took me half a crown back. I'm no fucking rabbit.

PATRICK  A rabbit?

PAUL  Someone that pays out for work.

BLOODY  And this morning the same little prick, Micka Kelly,
was doing the read and he didn't call me.

PATRICK  Because you didn't leave money?

BLOODY  Exactly, lad.

PAUL  Thought you said you were in a scrap?

BLOODY  Well I might have given him a clatter before I left
last night.

PAUL  You fuckin' eejit. Leavin' them short and givin' him a
clatter. What did you think would happen?

BLOODY  I don't care. I'm not payin' him or the bar man so
I can work tomorrow.

PATRICK  So if you just paid him and left, you'd be working
today?

BLOODY  Maybe, maybe not but I'm better than those rabbit
fucks. Disgraceful, they are.

PATRICK  It's work though.

BLOODY  I'm giving no backhanders, lad. I work as hard as any
man in that hatch.

PAUL  It goes on all the time. In every pub along the docks.

BLOODY  And they say it doesn't but you do see them with their
matchboxes. Fuckin' rabbits.

PAUL  Workin' as a floater has its drawbacks, Bloody. You have
to do something.

PATRICK  Are you a floater, Da?

**BLOODY**  He is. Like meself. You saw the gangs bein' called today. Prominent docker familys. With docker names. Doyle is a docker name, but you're not the right Doyle, lad. So you've to show your worth.

**PAUL**  Like Bloody here.

**BLOODY**  And your aul' fella.

**PATRICK**  You're both not working today.

**BLOODY**  Alright, we were just making a point.

**PAUL**  You can have your off days.

**BLOODY**  And some lads resort to other tactics.

**PAUL**  Other ways to get in.

**PATRICK**  Bribin'.

**PAUL**  Most lads buy a drink for the foreman/

**BLOODY**  Or givin' him your matchbox. Few shillings in it and then at the read tomorrow what's called?

**PATRICK**  Your name.

**PAUL**  Or a better chance of it anyway.

**BLOODY**  I've never done it and I never will, lad.

**PAUL**  What's your next call?

**BLOODY**  Ten o'clock read.

**PAUL**  At Palgrave?

**BLOODY**  Heiton's coal boat is coming in.

**PAUL**  Might chance that then. Me and the youngfella.

**BLOODY**  You should. Think it's Johnny Daly doing the read.

**PAUL**  Good man.

**BLOODY**  A fair man.

**PATRICK**  We trying it?

**PAUL** We are. We'll have another few pints. We'll need the energy.

**PATRICK** This was me first day and I soon came to know that the pub would be a regular stop in me life on the docks. The liquid food as they called it. These lads would mill the pints and go work on the ship. Unsuccessful at the first read, they'd go the pub and wait for the next. Do a day's work, get paid in the pubs and then head home. It was what kept some of the men going.

**PAUL** You right?

**PATRICK** Me and me Da headed to the ten o'clock read. A little blurry, if I'm honest.

**PAUL** Stay close to me.

**PATRICK** Right. Me Da talks to a few men around the crowd. Introduces me.

**VOICE** Alright, Little Paulie Doyle.

**VOICE** Spit of your aul' fella.

**PATRICK** They all shake me hand, nearly rip the arm from me socket. The strength of them.

**PAUL** Here we go.

**PATRICK** The stevedore steps forward and the crowd fall silent again. He starts calling the men for work. Some of the strangest names I've ever heard.

**VOICE** Joe the Goat.

**VOICE** Yeah.

**PATRICK** He walks forward.

**VOICE** Knees Murphy.

**PATRICK** He steps forward.

**VOICE** Ate The Babby.

**VOICE** Man Of A Thousand Faces.

**VOICE** The Wicked Chicken.

**VOICE** Buckets Of Blood.

**VOICE** Pen Luaidhe.

**VOICE** Beat The Dark.

**PATRICK** Mental names.

**VOICE** Bloody Hogg.

**PATRICK** Who we had a pint with.

**VOICE** By The Jingo.

**PATRICK** And so on. He calls twenty men from the read and amongst those names we hear.

**VOICE** Paulie Doyle.

**PATRICK** Me Da steps forward and he drops a nod towards me.

**VOICE** Little Paulie Doyle.

**PATRICK** Me.

**VOICE** That's it for today, men.

**PATRICK** And he walks away.

**PAUL** Look at you getting called out.

**PATRICK** Was that 'cause of you?

**PAUL** No, I was goin' to fuckin' leave you.

**PATRICK** Thanks.

**BLOODY** Howya, lads.

**PAUL** Howya. Guess we're both workin' today.

**BLOODY** The three of us. You're welcome, youngfella.

**PATRICK** Bloody put in a word with the foreman, he knew him. And me first job on the docks started.

**PAUL** Right, son. You ready?

**BLOODY** You become a man today, youngfella.

PATRICK  At the top of the hatch, we stood. A mountain of coal below us.

PAUL  Get your hat, son.

PATRICK  What?

BLOODY  Fuck it in at a tub and that's where you're working.

PAUL  Try for the edges.

BLOODY  Safer.

PAUL  One.

BLOODY  Two.

PAUL  Three.

PATRICK  Every man had a flat cap. For protection in the hold and to stake your claim to a work spot. In they went. Me Da got the edge, Bloody got the edge. Mine landed right in the middle.

BLOODY  You need to work on your aim, kid. Aim like a blind whore.

PAUL  I'll swap with you, son.

PATRICK  No, I'm alright.

PAUL  Grand.

BLOODY  Good on ya'!

PATRICK  We went into the hold. A collier as the ships were called.

PAUL  Here's your shovel.

PATRICK  A number seven they're called. A big fucking thing with a pointed end.

BLOODY  Four men to a tub, lad.

PAUL  We fill the tub and attach it to the crane.

PATRICK  And that would lift it out and onto the dock.

**BLOODY**  A full tub up and an empty tub down.

**PAUL**  You're with me and Bloody.

**BLOODY**  And Won't Go Home is the fourth.

**PATRICK**  Is that really what he's called?

**PAUL**  Yeah.

**BLOODY**  He hates the wife.

**PAUL**  Loves the coal.

**BLOODY**  Loves the long days.

**PAUL**  And won't go home.

**BLOODY**  Good worker, good man.

**PAUL**  Most of us have nicknames, son.

**PATRICK**  Yeah, I heard the names at the read.

**BLOODY**  Over there, that's The Bleeder and he's working with
Chicky May, Oxo Byrne and Diesel.

**PATRICK**  Diesel?

**PAUL**  Diesel do for the wife, Diesel do for the kids.

**BLOODY**  Good workers.

**PATRICK**  They all looked like they were smugglin' grapefruits in
their arms. We all stood on top a mountain of coal. Working
under our feet. Some men had different ways of doin' it.
The classic, just heavin' the coal in. All four men working
together. Other men dug down so the tubs could turn on
their side and they'd rawhead it in. Me Da and Bloody didn't
like that.

**PAUL**  It's easier but fuck that.

**BLOODY**  You're digging into the depths of the coal, lad. With
it all above you.

**PAUL**  Risk it avalanching down on top o' ya'.

**BLOODY**  That's not where you want to be. On the peas and beans, it's grand.

**PATRICK**  What?

**PAUL**  The peas and beans are smaller bits of coal, son. What we have today. Welsh, railway coal. And look at the size of the fuckers.

**PATRICK**  They were massive. Some the size of your head.

**BLOODY**  So we don't want that fallin' on us, lad. Too many ladies would miss aul' Bloody Hogg.

**PAUL**  Miss getting the diseases you're passin' about.

**BLOODY**  I'm as clean as a whistle.

**PAUL**  You're as clean as me hole.

**PATRICK**  And that was the day. Slaggin', windin' each other up. Made the day go faster. We shovelled coal after coal, filled tub after tub, it seemed like it was never endin'. And all the while, the shovel was gettin' heavier and heavier.

**PAUL**  You slowin' down, son?

**BLOODY**  Can't keep up with the aul'fella?

**PATRICK**  Just pacin' meself.

**BLOODY**  Yeah, yeah, lad. Your grip is all wrong.

**PAUL**  Don't grip it so tight.

**BLOODY**  Said that to many a lady.

**PAUL**  Needs to be looser in the hands.

**BLOODY**  You need a free-movin' grip. Your hands will be blistered off ya' in no time.

**PAUL**  Smooth and easy.

**PATRICK**  They helped a lot, showed me what you do and what you don't. But the blisters came anyway.

**BLOODY** Only one thing for that, lad. Go into the corner there and piss on your hands.

**PATRICK** As if I'd fall for that.

**PAUL** He's right.

**BLOODY** It helps.

**PAUL** Takes the sting out of them.

**PATRICK** Piss off.

**BLOODY** Good choice of words, lad. Now piss off into the corner.

**PAUL** Trust me, son. It helps. I've done it meself, many times.

**BLOODY** I even pissed on his hands once, when he couldn't go.

**PATRICK** That true?

**PAUL** Not me proudest moment.

**PATRICK** So I went into the corner, and pissed on me hands.

**BLOODY** Did it help?

**PATRICK** It did fuckin' help.

**PAUL** Eases the pain, now get back to the tub.

**PATRICK** The more we dug down, the deeper we went, the blacker we got. The coal dust thickened, coverin' us. So much that eventually I could only see a faint bit of light comin' into the hatch. Shovellin' in the dark for hours/

**BLOODY** Gets the blood goin', doesn't it, lad?

**PATRICK** I'm fuckin' wrecked.

**PAUL** You'll get used to it.

**BLOODY** You're goin' well for your first time.

**PAUL** Keep it up.

**PATRICK** I did and I put me shovel down and I hit somethin'.

**BLOODY** The bottom. Here, take this.

**PATRICK**  I was handed a square headed shovel.

**PAUL**  Easier to scoop it off the bottom, son.

**PATRICK**  We were nearly done. Tons and tons of coal gone and down to the last bit. We loaded the tub.

**BLOODY**  That's her full.

**PATRICK**  And up it went like the rest. We shovelled on. Until/

**PAUL**  Patrick, watch!

**PATRICK**  What?

**BLOODY**  Move, lad!

**PATRICK**  I looked up and I see a black ball fallin' towards me/

**PAUL**  Fuck!

**BLOODY**  Youngfella!

*Pause. He's hit by the falling coal.*

Is he dead?

**PAUL**  No, he's breathing. Son?

**BLOODY**  You sure he's not.

**PAUL**  Yeah, just a bad knock. He'll be alright.

**BLOODY**  Will I piss on him?

**PAUL**  Fucking stand over there, will ya'?

**BLOODY**  Just tryin' to help.

**PAUL**  Son?

**PATRICK**  I open me eyes and me Da and Bloody are over me. What happened?

**BLOODY**  Perk of the job.

**PAUL**  You took a piece of coal to the head.

**BLOODY**  You took it well.

**PAUL**  How you feelin'?

**PATRICK**  Like I took a piece of coal to the head.

**BLOODY**  But you took it well.

**PAUL**  Will you fuck off over there?

**BLOODY**  Fine.

**PATRICK**  An' me Da pulled me up. Bump on the head was the worst of me troubles.

**PAUL**  Always watch out for fallin' coal/

**PATRICK**  I learned that day.

**PAUL**  Some men don't wake up from knocks like that.

**BLOODY**  Not even with a little bit of piss.

**PATRICK**  When we came off the ship, I didn't recognise me Da or Bloody. Covered from head to toe. Black.

**BLOODY**  It's a good look. Come on, we get a pint into us.

**PATRICK**  Over to the pub. Where we were also goin' to be paid.

**PAUL**  Few pints, get paid and we go home to your mother.

**PATRICK**  And we waited. I have to say, after a long day in the dark, a pint was what I needed. And I didn't even know it. Around the pub, there were all the dockers waitin' to be paid. Waitin' for the foreman to come in. Piles of dust around our feet.

**VOICE**  Me bleedin' floor.

**BLOODY**  What d'ya want us to do? Been workin' hard all day.

**VOICE**  Now I've to work harder because you got work.

**BLOODY**  Piss off and give me a pint.

**VOICE**  I'll piss in your bleedin' pint.

**BLOODY**  Fuckin' dare ya'!

**PAUL**  You've a way with people, Bloody.

**BLOODY**  It's me charm. Nothin' like a few pints.

PAUL  Few pints and getting paid.

BLOODY  And I'm gettin' it all too. No paying for work tomorrow.

PAUL  It's Johnny Daly. You won't have to.

BLOODY  Better not.

PATRICK  A few pints down and Johnny Daly came in.

BLOODY  Here we go.

PATRICK  And we all got paid.

PAUL  Now, you're handin' some of that to your ma.

PATRICK  Course.

PAUL  And give me two shillings.

PATRICK  For what?

PAUL  Just do it.

PATRICK  And I did. We had a few more pints and Bloody told some tales.

BLOODY  You should have seen it, youngfella. There were fifteen of them around me.

PAUL  Five.

BLOODY  You weren't there. Fifteen.

PAUL  Five.

BLOODY  But the five of them were big. Dirty south siders they were, from Ringsend or something. They were starting on me because I'm Bloody Hogg of the north side.

PATRICK  Why?

BLOODY  Big rivalry between north and south of the Liffey. I don't feel right over there. They're sly, they'd stab you in the back for an extra shilling. I'm known, and they knew me. They jumped me on the way back from Lynch's Den.

PAUL  He loves a good brothel.

**BLOODY** I'd business over there.

**PAUL** Your mickey had business.

**BLOODY** Yeah, yeah. But I took on the fifteen/

**PAUL** Five/

**BLOODY** of them. One after the other. They didn't stand a chance. And what's the moral of the story?

**PAUL** That you can't fuckin' count.

**PATRICK** An' the ride isn't worth travellin' that far.

*PAUL laughs.*

**BLOODY** You cheeky little bastard.

**PATRICK** Thanks.

**BLOODY** Don't mess with Bloody Hogg. That's the moral of the story.

**PAUL** Here, I'd love to stay and hear the same stories. That coincidentally change every time I hear them but/

**BLOODY** Fuck off/

**PAUL** Good to see you, Bloody.

**PATRICK** See ya'.

**BLOODY** See ya', lads.

**PATRICK** We walk from the pub, as we do I see me Da pass something to the publican.

**PAUL** Give this to Johnny. From Paulie and Little Paulie Doyle.

**PATRICK** And we leave.

**PAUL** Proud of you, son. You did well today.

**PATRICK** What did you give him?

**PAUL** What?

**PATRICK** Is that what you wanted the two shillings for?

PAUL  It's just for tomorrow. Until we get in with him and show our worth. The strength of the Doyle men, what?

PATRICK  But Bloody said?

PAUL  Bloody is an old timer. He doesn't have to for work, and soon enough, we won't have to either.

PATRICK  Alright, Da.

PAUL  Let's get home.

PATRICK  Behind us, the pub door flies open.

BLOODY  Here!

PATRICK  It's Bloody.

BLOODY  You bleedin' rabbit!

PAUL  Go back inside, Bloody.

BLOODY  You and your little rabbit. What did you drop behind the bar there?

PAUL  None of your business.

BLOODY  It is my business. I get you and your little rabbit work and this is how you pay me back? Backhanders so you'll be working tomorrow and I won't?

PAUL  You know the lads, I don't.

BLOODY  Don't give me that fuckin' shit. You're a disgrace.

PATRICK  Bloody just kept walkin'. And me Da didn't move. Until they were face to face.

BLOODY  Stealin' work from me.

PATRICK  Bloody swung for me Da. Missed.

PAUL  I don't want to fight you, Bloody. It's something I had to do.

PATRICK  I stepped forward.

PAUL  Get back, Patrick. I have this.

PATRICK  As Bloody swung again.

BLOODY  Prick!

PAUL  Me bleedin' jaw.

PATRICK  Landin' this time.

BLOODY  Thought you were a man of honour, Paulie.

PAUL  Don't make me put you down.

BLOODY  Come on, you prick.

PATRICK  An' they went for each other. Blow after blow. As people on the street started to notice.

WOMAN  Jaysus, they're killin' each other.

PATRICK  Blow after blow.

WOMAN  Stop them!

PATRICK  Neither man fallin'.

WOMAN  Youngfella, stop them!

PATRICK  I can't.

WOMAN  I'm callin' the police.

PATRICK  Da, stop.

PAUL  You prick!

PATRICK  That's enough.

BLOODY  Fuck you!

PATRICK  Da! They didn't stop. I ran in.

BLOODY  I'll kill the two o'ya'.

PAUL  Get back, son.

PATRICK  He threw me back.

PAUL  Get out of the way. I have this handled.

PATRICK  As he's lookin' at me. Bloody cracks me Da over the back of the head.

**BLOODY**  You fuckin' prick!

**PATRICK**  And me Da falls to the ground. Smashes his head on the footpath. I run to him. Da. Open your eyes. There are screams from the street.

**WOMAN**  Jesus Christ.

**BLOODY**  Fuck.

**WOMAN**  Is he okay?

**PATRICK**  Da.

**WOMAN**  Someone help!

**PATRICK**  Da!

**WOMAN**  He's bleedin'. Get a doctor!

*Pause.*

**PATRICK**  He never opened his eyes again. The aftermath is a blur. Just voices and screams on the street.

**VOICE**  Jesus Christ.

**VOICE**  Bloody murdered him.

**VOICE**  The youngfella didn't even help.

**VOICE**  It was vicious.

**VOICE**  They were tearing chunks from each other.

**VOICE**  Blood was everywhere.

**VOICE**  Heard Bloody did a runner.

**VOICE**  He's in the wind.

**VOICE**  He died in his son's arms.

**VOICE**  Fuckin' tragic.

**PATRICK**  The next thing I remember was me ma.

**MARY**  Son/

**PATRICK**  She gave me a big hug/

**MARY** You poor thing/

**PATRICK** I didn't know what to say/

**MARY** Your poor father/

**PATRICK** He wouldn't let me help/

**MARY** Paul Doyle, you drunken fool/

**PATRICK** He wasn't drunk, Ma/

**MARY** May God have mercy on his soul.

**PATRICK** She was angry.

**MARY** I can't believe this.

**PATRICK** They didn't catch Bloody.

**MARY** That scumbag.

**PATRICK** He vanished. Heard rumours that he hopped a boat to England. Me Da was buried. In Glasnevin. We didn't have the money but they did a whip around for him. He was buried and that was that.

**MARY** You're the man of the house now, son.

**PATRICK** Yeah, Ma.

**MARY** Don't worry. We'll get through this together.

**PATRICK** My Ma was the best woman I'd ever met. She never complained. I was their only child. I was their only child. I was the youngest.

**MARY** These are the times we live in, darling.

**PATRICK** I'm sorry you've lost another person you love, Ma.

**MARY** Don't be sorry. It's God's will. And I still have you, don't I?

**PATRICK** You'll always have me, Ma.

**MARY** Until some beautiful girl comes and sweeps you off your feet.

**PATRICK** Never. And we got on with it. I became known on the docks. Little Paulie Doyle and it stuck. For a year or so, I worked mostly coal. In 1939, we took a big hit. World War Two had started. I was seventeen. During that time, I continued to work on the docks. Gettin' work here and there as many left. Some joined the British Army, some left for sea but I stayed, like many. Was a hard few years. Boats going missin', boats getting torpedoed. My Ma got a job as a house maid, and we just about covered the rent and kept ourselves fed. She was my sole priority over those years. Makin' sure she was okay, and provided for. The war years passed. And Irishmen flooded back home. All lookin' for work. Some lifetime dockers, most not. So in 1947 a trade union list of full-time dockers was drawn up. And they were given first preference at the read. Your status indicated by a button. I applied and got mine. Some didn't.

VOICE  I have to get a button to get a job?

PATRICK  It meant a better chance at work.

VOICE  No way, I've been down here me whole life.

PATRICK  Lifetime dockers too stubborn to register.

VOICE  Fuckin' disgraceful!

PATRICK  They fell behind. Buttonmen worked first, called first at each read. And at the end of the read the foreman would say/

VOICE  Any more buttonmen?

PATRICK  If there wasn't. Non-buttonmen then got called. It was a mistake not to register.

VOICE  Now I'm never goin' to be picked for work.

PATRICK  They grew to regret their choice.

VOICE  Come on, you know me. I'm here me whole life.

VOICE  Sorry, Mitten. I've to call the buttonmen first.

VOICE  Please, I need to feed me children.

PATRICK  As if the read could demoralise a man any more. I'd look at those men and your heart went out to them. And the next few years, it was me and me ma. Work was good. So we could live better.

*As* **PATRICK** *talks, we start to hear* **VOICES** *from the streets coming through.*

**VOICE**  You comin' to the dance?

**VOICE**  I've heard they're the best craic.

**PATRICK**  I started to head out more.

**VOICE**  Ah come on.

**PATRICK**  To some of the dance halls poppin' up all over Dublin.

**VOICE**  Would you like to dance?

**PATRICK**  Young men, young women, went out on the town.

**VOICE**  I'm going to ask her to dance tonight.

**PATRICK**  And many found love.

**VOICE**  I hope he asks me tonight.

**PATRICK**  That lasted forever.

**VOICE**  I'd love to.

**PATRICK**  And I was one.

   **PATRICK** *leaves.*

**VOICE**  Right, get in line, will ya'!

**ESTHER**  All the girls paid themselves in back then.

**VOICE**  Four pence.

**ESTHER**  As did the men.

**VOICE**  Sixpence for the gents.

**ESTHER**  And Jaysus, it was packed.

**VOICE**  Here, you. Sixpence, come on.

**VOICE**  Alright, fuckin' relax.

   *Lights change to* **ESTHER**. *1955.*

**ESTHER** I hadn't been to a dance hall before. Twenty-five and I've never been to a dance hall. But Margo wouldn't take no for an answer.

**MARGO** You are comin'.

**ESTHER** I don't want to go.

**MARGO** Want to end up an old maid, do you?

**ESTHER** Dance halls aren't the only place to meet men.

**MARGO** I know that, but they're the best.

**ESTHER** You'd know.

**MARGO** I would. You can meet them elsewhere but here/

**ESTHER** What?

**MARGO** Here they get to see ya'/

**ESTHER** See ya'? They can see ya' anywhere.

**MARGO** Here, they *see ya'*. What you move like, dance like, get to see what they like.

**ESTHER** You've no shame.

**MARGO** Leave the shame to the nuns.

**ESTHER** You're definitely no nun.

**MARGO** Don't be jealous. I'll show you the ropes.

**ESTHER** Ropes? Jaysus, I'm not into this.

**MARGO** Ah relax. The ropes, I'll teach you.

**ESTHER** If you're so good, how come you have nobody yet?

**MARGO** Lookin' for the right one is all.

**ESTHER** Yeah, sure.

**MARGO** Come on, Saint Bridget.

**ESTHER** Margo was full on. She didn't care what anyone thought. Her parents were dead and she had no family. No one to answer to. If I went dancin' around actin' like that? Me Ma would crease me, and then me Nan would crease me.

**MARGO**  Come on.

**ESTHER**  I am.

**MARGO**  I'll show you everythin' I know.

**ESTHER**  You're too kind.

**MARGO**  It's simple. They'll stand over across the way, like they're afraid of us. But we don't pay no mind to them. We dance and if one likes you, he'll come over and ask you to dance. Got it?

**ESTHER**  Don't know, Margo. Sounds very complicated.

**MARGO**  I'll choke that sarcasm out of you.

**ESTHER**  I'm messin'.

**MARGO**  And as I said, I'm here to help you.

**ESTHER**  Thanks, Margo.

**MARGO**  Oh, look at him.

**ESTHER**  Margo.

**MARGO**  Relax, I'll be back in a minute.

**ESTHER**  And she left me. But I did what little she said. I danced and enjoyed meself as the music played through the night. The hall had it all. People that were single.

**VOICE**  Would you like to dance?

**VOICE**  I'd love to.

**ESTHER**  People that weren't as single.

**VOICE**  Were you dancin' with that girl?

**VOICE**  Just a little.

**VOICE**  I swear to God.

**VOICE**  I'm sorry, love.

ESTHER  Margo was jivin' her little heart out.

VOICE  Go on, do it.

PATRICK  I will.

VOICE  Don't be a fuckin' chicken.

PATRICK  Piss off.

ESTHER  And then a voice spoke to me. With the most romantic introduction ever.

PATRICK  Howya.

*Pause.*

ESTHER  Hello.

PATRICK  Do you want to dance?

ESTHER  I'd love to. I'm Esther.

PATRICK  Patrick Doyle.

ESTHER  Very formal, Patrick Doyle.

PATRICK  Not the best at askin' good-lookin' girls to dance.

ESTHER  Sure you're not. And we danced. He was gorgeous. Big strong fella.

PATRICK  Oh, sorry.

ESTHER  But not the best dancer.

PATRICK  Sorry.

ESTHER  Kept standin' on me feet.

PATRICK  Shite.

ESTHER  Language.

PATRICK  Sorry, I'm shite...I'm rubbish at dancin'.

ESTHER  You're not as bad as you think.

MARGO  Would you look at her!

ESTHER  Shut up, Margo.

**MARGO**  Go on, girl.

**PATRICK**  Friend of yours?

**MARGO**  Doesn't take long to get the hang of it, does it?

**ESTHER**  Unfortunately.

**PATRICK**  She's off her head.

**ESTHER**  You've no idea.

**MARGO**  Jaysus, he's massive.

**ESTHER**  Margo!

**MARGO**  I'll leave you to it. An' don't be afraid to put the hips into it, you're not at mass.

**ESTHER**  We danced all night. The standin' on me toes stopped and soon enough so did the music.

**VOICE**  You ready, we head home?

**VOICE**  Yeah, let's go.

**VOICE**  Good luck.

**ESTHER**  And everyone started to leave.

**PATRICK**  Can I walk you home?

**ESTHER**  I'd like that.

**PATRICK**  So would I.

**ESTHER**  We left.

**MARGO**  I'll talk to you tomorrow, right? Tell me everythin'.

**ESTHER**  Margo left.

**PATRICK**  So where would I be walkin' you to?

**ESTHER**  Dominick Street.

**PATRICK**  It's on me way.

**ESTHER**  If it wasn't, would you still walk me?

**PATRICK**  Nah.

ESTHER  Thought as much. Where are you livin' then?

PATRICK  Railway Street.

ESTHER  Ah, the Monto.

PATRICK  Guilty.

ESTHER  All that carry on is gone a while though, isn't it?

PATRICK  Yeah, not long after I was born, me Ma says.

ESTHER  So what age would Patrick Doyle of the Monto be?

PATRICK  I'll be thirty-three in November.

ESTHER  Have to say. Wouldn't have guessed that. A bit old to
be chasin' girls, aren't we?

PATRICK  Maybe so. It's rude for a gentleman to ask a lady her
age.

ESTHER  Ask away so.

PATRICK  Good one.

ESTHER  He was a gentleman. In every sense of the word. He
walked me home. We talked, we laughed and I didn't want
it to end.

PATRICK  How come I haven't seen you at the dance halls before?

ESTHER  Me Da wasn't well, so meself and me sisters had to
work a lot.

PATRICK  To help out.

ESTHER  Yeah.

PATRICK  What happened to your Da?

ESTHER  He had cancer.

PATRICK  Had, so he's/

ESTHER  Dead?

PATRICK  Was going to say better.

ESTHER  Ah right.

**PATRICK** So he is better?

**ESTHER** No.

**PATRICK** Oh.

**ESTHER** He died last year.

**PATRICK** Sorry to hear.

**ESTHER** He worked with coal. Breathing in all the soot. Lung cancer.

**PATRICK** That's reassuring.

**ESTHER** What?

**PATRICK** I'm a docker.

**ESTHER** Great.

**PATRICK** On the coal boats mostly.

**ESTHER** Oh.

**PATRICK** Yeah.

**ESTHER** Risk of the job, I guess.

**PATRICK** Along with hundreds more.

    *Pause.*

    This is an uplifting conversation, isn't it?

**ESTHER** You're a smooth one, Patrick Doyle.

**PATRICK** Cancer and coal.

**ESTHER** All a girl could want on a first date. Is your father a docker?

**PATRICK** He was.

**ESTHER** Was...your father's dead too, isn't he?

**PATRICK** He is.

**ESTHER** And the mood continues to lighten.

**PATRICK** It's a part of life.

**ESTHER** What happened to him?

**PATRICK** He was in a fight. Fell and hit his head.

**ESTHER** That must've been awful news to get.

**PATRICK** He was in me arms when he died.

**ESTHER** Oh God.

**PATRICK** Some people do the whole, I like you, I like you too, I'd love to see you again, I'd love to see you again too. Not us. My Da's dead, cancer! My Da's dead too, murder!

*They both laugh and smile at each other.*

**ESTHER** My Da is dead. Cancer.

**PATRICK** My Da is dead too. Murder.

**ESTHER** And I do like you.

**PATRICK** I like you too.

**ESTHER** And I'd love to see you again.

**PATRICK** I'd love to see you again too.

**ESTHER** And we got to me house.

**PATRICK** Sorry about standin' all over your feet tonight.

**ESTHER** It's grand. Next time, you'll be better.

**PATRICK** I will.

**ESTHER** Good night, Patrick.

**PATRICK** Good night, Esther.

**ESTHER** We agreed to go the pictures the following Sunday. And it went from there. Seeing him more, caring about him more. He was the best man I'd ever met. Then I met his mother, Mary.

**MARY** So you're the beautiful lady that's stolen my son away from me.

**ESTHER** I'm afraid so.

MARY  He's a lucky man. How did you get her, son?

PATRICK  I couldn't tell you, Ma. Same way I couldn't tell you how I got you as a ma.

ESTHER  Mary lit up when he said that. He didn't seem like the men of those days. He was strong, you can tell that, but he had a gentle side. He cared and he looked after everyone he loved. And I became one of them. We were walking back from a dance one night, he was walking me home. And he stopped. Is everything okay?

PATRICK  Esther, will you marry me?

ESTHER  I nearly died. But we did. That winter, 1956. We married and there was a hoolie the likes I'd never seen. There was a community hall on Railway Street and Mary knew the fella that ran it.

MARY  It's me son's wedding.

VOICE  What do you need?

MARY  Just the room. We'll bring the rest.

ESTHER  Everyone piled in. Crates of whiskey. Singing, dancing and the craic.

PATRICK  Ladies and gentlemen.

VOICE  Sit down, you.

VOICE  You drunken eejit!

PATRICK  You shut your mouth.

VOICE  Or what?

MARY  Or I'll reef you out that door.

VOICE  Sorry, Mary.

MARGO  Go on, Patrick.

ESTHER  Margo, would you let him speak.

MARGO  Jaysus, that's the thanks I get. I introduced you two.

ESTHER You left me on me own in a dance hall.

MARGO After teaching you everything I know.

ESTHER Thanks, Margo.

MARGO You're welcome. Go for it, Patrick.

PATRICK I just wanted to thank you all for comin'.

VOICE Well you had whiskey.

MARY Get him out.

VOICE Ah no, Mary. I'm sorry.

PATRICK And to my beautiful bride. What can I say?

ESTHER You better say bleedin' somethin'!

VOICE Sing us an aul' song, Paulie. Get the party goin'.

PATRICK Sing. Fuck off.

ESTHER You afraid?

PATRICK Alright. I've been known to belt out a song or two in the hatch.

VOICE The poor fuckers havin' to listen.

PATRICK Well you poor fuckers are next.

PATRICK *sings, as he starts the rest all join in.*

ESTHER There were sore heads in the north inner city for months after that wedding. We moved in with Mary, she was happy to have us. I worked in Jacob's biscuit factory at the time but once you got married, you weren't allowed to work.

MAN Esther, is it true what I heard?

ESTHER Depends what you heard, sir.

MAN We heard you got married, Esther.

ESTHER Ah no, who told you that?

MAN Some of the staff said they were at your wedding.

ESTHER  Some of the staff need to stop dippin' into their whiskey before work, sir.

MAN  So you're not married?

ESTHER  Not that I know of, sure, who'd have me?

MAN  Okay, I'll follow up on it with those telling lies.

PATRICK  Did he make you leave?

ESTHER  I told him I wasn't married.

PATRICK  Ashamed of me, are you?

ESTHER  We need the money.

PATRICK  He'll get you eventually.

ESTHER  Yeah but I'll have a little more wages under me belt.

PATRICK  Esther Doyle, the little criminal.

ESTHER  I kept him off me back for a couple of months.

MAN  Esther?

ESTHER  Yes, sir.

MAN  May I speak with you a moment.

ESTHER  Of course.

MAN  You're married, Esther.

ESTHER  No, I'm not.

MAN  To a man named Patrick Doyle.

ESTHER  Never heard of him.

MAN  He works on the docks.

ESTHER  Never been the docks in me life.

MAN  And you live together on Railway Street.

ESTHER  Okay, you got me. We're newly-weds.

MAN  I heard you're married eight months.

ESTHER What are you, a detective?

MAN As you know, we don't allow married women to work/

ESTHER I know.

MAN Congratulations/

ESTHER You're too kind.

MAN We wish you all the best with your life and here is a little parting gift.

ESTHER A cake.

MAN A sponge cake. Best of luck.

ESTHER That's all you got when they let you go. Married women had to go and be housewives, that's just the way it was and that's what I did. A load of bollocks.

PATRICK Al Capone gets caught, what?

ESTHER This is your fault.

PATRICK Didn't ask you to say yes.

ESTHER Outside of work, everything was good. We were happily married and in 1958/

PATRICK Ma, Esther's goin' into labour!

ESTHER Patrick!

PATRICK Bollocks, bollocks, bollocks. Don't worry, we'll get you to the hospital.

MARY She's not going to make it to the hospital.

PATRICK I'll stick her on the bike. Be grand.

MARY Cop on.

PATRICK I'll pedal like there's no tomorrow.

MARY Her water just broke. The baby is comin'.

PATRICK The baby's comin', comin' where?

MARY Out of her.

PATRICK  Jesus, ma.

MARY  Listen, go get Mrs Plunkett. Tell her what's happening.

ESTHER  He legged it. He came back.

PATRICK  Mrs Plunkett isn't there! She's not there! What'll I do?

ESTHER  It'll be okay.

PATRICK  You're right, it will be okay.

ESTHER  Oh Jesus Christ.

PATRICK  You're goin' to be okay, Esther. Isn't she, Ma?

MARY  Just get out of me way.

PATRICK  Okay. Right, Esther. Breathe.

ESTHER  I am breathin'.

MARY  Push.

ESTHER  I am pushin'.

MARY  Push harder.

ESTHER  I can't.

MARY  You can.

ESTHER  I can't.

PATRICK  You can.

ESTHER  Shut up, Patrick!

PATRICK  Okay.

ESTHER  You did this to me.

PATRICK  You make it sound like it's a bad thing.

ESTHER  Fuck you.

PATRICK  Language.

ESTHER  Go to hell!

MARY  Push, darling. Son?

PATRICK  Yeah?

MARY  Stand over there, you're in the way.

ESTHER  And he did. Mary was unbelievable.

MARY  One last push!

PATRICK  Is that crying, I hear?

ESTHER  And he was here. A gorgeous little thing.

PATRICK  What is it?

MARY  You did great, darling.

PATRICK  It's a boy!

ESTHER  Mary kisses me on the head and I close my eyes.

PATRICK  Is she okay?

MARY  She's sleepin'.

PATRICK  Are you sure? Is she breathin'?

MARY  Here.

ESTHER  I open my eyes and I see Patrick holdin' Francis.

MARY  The spit of his father.

PATRICK  You think?

MARY  I do.

ESTHER  A doctor arrived shortly after and checked on me.
I was fine and so was Francis. I don't talk; I just lay there.

MARY  He's beautiful.

PATRICK  Ma, I would've been lost without you.

MARY  I know.

PATRICK  Where'd you even/

MARY  I've delivered many babies into this world. It's what we
all did in our day, and still today when we're needed.

PATRICK  You're incredible, Ma.

**MARY**  No, I'm not.

**PATRICK**  Yes, you are. This little fella, Ma. Will want for nothin', I'll protect him and let no harm fall on that beautiful little head. Like what Da did for me. Pushed me away, so I'd be safe.

**MARY**  Your father was just doin' what any parent would do. What's best for their child.

**PATRICK**  I know he was.

**ESTHER**  And Mary placed her hand on his.

**PATRICK**  Are you okay?

*Pause.*

**MARY**  There's something I need to tell you.

**PATRICK**  What's wrong?

**MARY**  Just listen, okay? I'm...not your mother. I raised you from birth but I am not your mother.

**PATRICK** *goes to speak but* **MARY** *keeps talking.*

**PATRICK**  What/

**MARY**  Please, just listen. I delivered you, just like I did with little Francis. You were born to a woman called Anne Brady. She was a country girl and one of the poor unfortunate girls of the Monto. She left you on our door and we raised you as our own. Me and your father, Lord rest him.

**PATRICK**  Come on, Ma. That can't be true.

**MARY**  It is, son. We took you in and l never looked back. You needed us and you were the most beautiful little thing/

**PATRICK**  I'm going to head out for a bit.

**ESTHER**  He kissed both of us and then kissed Francis.

**MARY**  Son?

**PATRICK**  Don't worry, Ma. I'm okay. Just need a walk is all.

MARY I'm sorry. I should have/

PATRICK You gave me a life when someone else couldn't. I love you and you'll always be me ma.

ESTHER He smiled and he left. Are you okay, Mary?

MARY Yeah. Just somethin' I've always wanted to tell him. I didn't even plan on doin' it there, it just came out.

ESTHER He worships the ground you walk on, you know that.

MARY He's a good man.

ESTHER Because of you. And Paul. You didn't have to take him in.

MARY Oh we did. It was freezin' that day, snowin' an' all.

ESTHER Did you know his mother?

MARY Just from bein' around the Monto. She was a lovely girl, beautiful-lookin' and she did what a lot of women did in that situation.

ESTHER Couldn't imagine givin' up my child.

MARY Sometimes we have to think of what's best for the child/

ESTHER And she was right.

MARY He's the best thing that ever happened to us.

ESTHER And we just spoke for hours, about everythin'. Patrick came back a few hours later with a few drinks on him. You alright, love?

PATRICK She was a prostitute, Esther. I'm here because some fella knocked up a prostitute and even she didn't want me.

ESTHER Don't think like that/

PATRICK I thought I came from a lovin', carin' family/

ESTHER You do/

PATRICK I'm a bastard. Dropped at the door of strangers because she didn't love me/

ESTHER  She did love you, that's why she did it.

PATRICK  Givin' me to strangers?

ESTHER  Strangers that loved you, raised you and made you the man you are today.

PATRICK  I love me Ma and Da, love them. But I can't help but think, why?

ESTHER  I know and we will never know why. What we do know is that you're here. Mary and Paul loved you and you're their son.

*Pause.*

PATRICK  I'm their son.

ESTHER  And he rested on me. That was the only time he mentioned what happened and never again. We lived, Francis grew but no children followed. They just didn't happen and we were lucky to have been blessed with him. Life was tough but we got by. You had to. And we lived on Railway Street until 1964, when we got a house out in Coolock. Francis was delighted, fields, open spaces to play in but Patrick wasn't too happy. Himself and many other dockers that were moved from the city.

*As* ESTHER *talks, we start to hear* VOICES *from elsewhere coming through.*

VOICE  That's fuckin' miles away.

VOICE  There's nothin' out there but fields.

ESTHER  He felt it was out in the countryside.

VOICE  Into the bleedin' wilderness.

ESTHER  And many agreed.

VOICE  I can't do it.

ESTHER  Too far from the docks.

VOICE  I'm movin' back in.

**ESTHER**  And it was too quiet.

**VOICE**  You shut up, we're not.

**ESTHER**  But he got used to it.

**VOICE**  Fine.

**ESTHER**  We all did.

> **ESTHER** *leaves.*

**VOICE**  I'm never goin' to like it.

**PATRICK**  That's what we all said.

**VOICE**  It's the middle of nowhere.

**PATRICK**  'Cause it fuckin' was at the time.

**VOICE**  I'm goin' mad out here.

**PATRICK**  Jaysus, I'd been livin' out there six years already.

**VOICE**  I'm goin' to be a fuckin' culchie.

**VOICE**  Be cows lookin' at me in the bath an' all.

> *Lights change to* **PATRICK**. *1970.*

**PATRICK**  Once I got over being in the country, it was grand. Cycled in to the docks every day, was super bleedin' fit. Today, I'm workin' with me mate, Whacker. He only just moved out to Coolock. Bit younger than me but he's great craic.

**WHACKER**  Little Paulie, I'm not built for the countryside.

**PATRICK**  You'll live. Come on, we get this hook.

**WHACKER**  Fuckin' hate fresh air.

**PATRICK**  We were workin' on a timber boat and Whacker forgot his hook.

**WHACKER**  We'll be two minutes.

**PATRICK**  We better be.

**WHACKER**  We don't have to be at the hatch for half an hour.

PATRICK  We went to his Ma's flat. To grab a spare hook.

WHACKER  I'll be back in a minute.

PATRICK  I wait. I turn around. There's a young fella behind me. You alright?

BILL  No.

PATRICK  What you lookin' for?

BILL  The ship.

PATRICK  Well it's not fuckin' here.

BILL  You're working the ship I'm on but I lost me way and couldn't remember where it's docked.

PATRICK  So you thought it'd be down here in the flats.

BILL  You were there. So I thought you knew.

PATRICK  You can come with us, youngfella. He's just gettin' a hook.

BILL  His hook?

PATRICK  Whacker?

*Pause.*

WHACKER  What?

PATRICK  Bring another hook.

WHACKER  Grand.

PATRICK  Whacker came down and the three of us headed to the ship.

WHACKER  First day, youngfella?

BILL  Second.

PATRICK  Da's button?

BILL  Yeah.

PATRICK  Who was your Da?

**BILL** Davey Kelly.

**PATRICK** Good man. Good worker. And I brought the kid with us. Showed him the ropes. He needed it. We got onto the ship with the other lads.

**WHACKER** Lads, this is Miss The Boat.

**BILL** What?

**VOICE** Howya, Miss The Boat.

**BILL** I'm Bill.

**PATRICK** Not anymore, youngfella.

**BILL** Ah fuck's sake.

**WHACKER** You'll get used to it.

**PATRICK** We were on a timber boat so the kid needed a hook.

**BILL** How do I use this thing?

**WHACKER** The timber is loose, and lifting that up with your bare hands, all day, your back would be gone.

**PATRICK** So you use your hook to pull them up.

**WHACKER** Then we tie a pile together and it goes up with the crane, right?

**BILL** Got it.

**PATRICK** This timber came from Russia. I worked many before. The kid has a tough day ahead of him.

**BILL** Jesus.

**PATRICK** That's our hatch for the day, youngfella. Come on. In we went.

**BILL** Was it snowing last night?

**WHACKER** Packed in Russia. Does be snowin' when they load it in.

**BILL** It's freezin'.

**WHACKER**  The nipples will be rock hard, lad.

**BILL**  You can't work in this.

**WHACKER**  Think you have it bad? Look.

**BILL**  Are they footprints?

**PATRICK**  The women that pack the timber pack it in their bare feet.

**WHACKER**  So grow a set.

**BILL**  It's like workin' in a fuckin' fridge.

**WHACKER**  Your little dick gettin' smaller?

**BILL**  I'll ask your Ma later.

**WHACKER**  You little bollocks.

**PATRICK**  That's it; don't let that fucker slag ya'.

**WHACKER**  Little fuck.

**PATRICK**  And we showed the kid the ropes. Help him out. Here, that singer-out sounds familiar.

**BILL**  The what?

**WHACKER**  The singer out, the fella at the top of the hatch. The crane man's eyes 'cause he can't see into the hatch.

**PATRICK**  He calls out.

**WHACKER**  Sings out.

**PATRICK**  So you don't get a smack of a crane.

**WHACKER**  Usually old, respected dockers. Ninety, some of them are.

**BILL**  Jaysus.

**WHACKER**  Yep, so respect them.

**PATRICK**  I tried to look up but I couldn't see his face.

**WHACKER**  Here.

PATRICK  What?

WHACKER  Get your head back down here, we've work to do.

PATRICK  Just recognise that singer-out.

WHACKER  Well you can kiss him after.

PATRICK  We worked the hatch until there wasn't a piece of timber left.

WHACKER  Come on, we get paid, kid.

BILL  We goin' the pub?

WHACKER  Nah, they paid you there back in Little Paulie's day.

PATRICK  The company's office now, lad. And as we walked into the office. I saw a face. A face of a man I knew from many years ago. Standin' in the office picking up his wages. The singer out I'd recognised. Must be fuckin' ninety at this rate. Bloody Hogg, smilin', laughin'.

WHACKER  You alright, Little Paulie?

*Pause.*

Little Paulie?

PATRICK  Yeah, I'm grand.

WHACKER  Sure? Look like you saw a ghost. Or you just shit yourself. You didn't shit yourself, did ya'?

PATRICK  No.

WHACKER  'Cause I'm not cleanin' that up/

PATRICK  Shut the fuck up, will you? We get paid and everyone leaves. Bloody walks down the Liffey.

WHACKER  I'll see you tomorrow, yeah?

PATRICK  Yeah.

BILL  Thanks for today, Little Paulie.

PATRICK  No bother. See you tomorrow, Miss The Boat.

**BILL**  I really am stuck with that fuckin' name.

**WHACKER**  Until the day you die. Which could be tomorrow, dangerous aul' job we do, youngfella.

**PATRICK**  And I follow Bloody. He heads into town. To a pub no doubt. He heads down a lane and I call him. Bloody? He stops and then continues walkin'. Bloody Hogg? He turns around.

*We only hear* **BLOODY**.

**BLOODY**  Sorry, lad. I think you've got me mixed up with someone else.

**PATRICK**  I know it's you.

**BLOODY**  I hate to disappoint you/

**PATRICK**  You're old, going by a new name but I know it's you.

**BLOODY**  My name is Jim Murphy. Not new, I've had it me whole life.

**PATRICK**  You don't remember me, do you?

**BLOODY**  Met many faces over the years, lad.

**PATRICK**  Do you remember a man called, Paulie Doyle?

**BLOODY**  Can't say that I do.

**PATRICK**  Do you remember his son? We all worked as coalies together.

**BLOODY**  I've to go, you've me confused with someone else.

**PATRICK**  I don't think I do. As he walks away. It all comes rushin' back. The fight, me Da, the cunt smackin' him over the head. I grab him.

**BLOODY**  What the fuck are you doin'?

**PATRICK**  Push him up against the wall.

**BLOODY**  Get your fuckin' hands off me.

**PATRICK**  What you goin' to do, kill me?

**BLOODY**  Get your *fuckin'* hands off me!

**PATRICK**  You killed my father, Bloody, and you're going to pay for it.

**BLOODY**  Stop.

**PATRICK**  I punch him across the face.

**BLOODY**  Please.

**PATRICK**  And again.

**BLOODY**  I'm an old man, please.

**PATRICK**  I don't stop. I hit him.

**BLOODY**  Please.

**PATRICK**  Hit him.

**BLOODY**  I'm sorry.

**PATRICK**  Hit him.

**BLOODY**  Please, Little Paulie.

**PATRICK**  I stop. What did ya' say?

**BLOODY**  I'm sorry. That day, things got out of hand.

**PATRICK**  He's dead because of you.

**BLOODY**  I didn't mean it. I was drunk, we were both at it.

**PATRICK**  I should kill you.

**BLOODY**  I think life is goin' to do that soon enough, lad.

**PATRICK**  I never want to see you again. If I do, I swear to God, I'll kill you.

**BLOODY**  You'll never see me face again.

**PATRICK**  As I'm walkin' away.

**BLOODY**  Run along little rabbit.

**PATRICK**  I turn, grab him and pin him against the wall.

**BLOODY**  Little Paulie/

**PATRICK**  Never let me see you again. I fucking mean it.

*Pause.*

I walk away, home and back to the docks the next mornin'.

**WHACKER**  Jaysus, did you hear?

**PATRICK**  What?

**WHACKER**  The aul' fella on the ship yesterday.

**PATRICK**  Who?

**WHACKER**  The singer-out, he was battered.

**PATRICK**  Jaysus. Is he alright?

**WHACKER**  He was taken to hospital last night.

*Pause.*

You said you knew him, didn't you?

**PATRICK**  Thought I did. Thought he was a friend of my Da.

**WHACKER**  And he wasn't?

**PATRICK**  No. Poor fella.

**WHACKER**  Yeah, the lads were saying he was battered.

**PATRICK**  Do they know who did it?

**WHACKER**  No, they didn't say.

**PATRICK**  And they never did. Bloody never came back to the docks and I never set eyes on him again. I got on with things. Grew older, changed. As did the job. First came decasualisation on the docks. When we finally got some sort of wage if we didn't work. Eighteen pounds. And if you worked, you got your day's pay. And the days of the traditional read/

**VOICE**  Murphy.

**VOICE**  Behan.

**VOICE**  Carrick.

VOICE  McDermott.

VOICE  Hawkins.

VOICE  Nevin/

PATRICK  Those days were gone. The read became centralised at Ocean Pier Gate and they started to rotate and call us alphabetically. If you worked today, tomorrow you went to the bottom of the list. Docker gangs broke up. You're now working with a man you might hate. And your choice of ship site and commodity was gone. Individuality was gone. Our freedom of movement for work was gone. And soon the writing was on the wall for us.

WHACKER  Jaysus, look at the door on this thing.

PATRICK  I've never seen a ship like that.

WHACKER  The doors are openin'.

PATRICK  Forklifts are driving out with the cargo.

WHACKER  What the fuck are they going to need us for?

PATRICK  I guess we'll see, Whacker.

*The lights slowly change and* ESTHER *walks out. 2019. The coffin is on the floor as before.*

ESTHER  Patrick could see it comin'. As could many of the men on the docks. Soon, containers were the way it all went and the docker, was no more. Those men that waited in the cold, early mornings all along the docks were gone. Machines with the strength of a hundred men were now in their place. Joined by coffee shops, business men in suits and a ship outside the Custom House is a thing of the past. The community, the friendship, it's all gone. Patrick retired in 1987 after forty-nine years on the docks. Mary passed that same year, at eighty-seven years young, missed by all. Patrick was lost when she died but soon, little voices began to take up his days and he became a new man.

SHARON  Granda, come on.

KIM  It's your turn, Granda.

STEPHEN  You've to catch us.

PATRICK  I'm too old for this shit, kids.

SHARON  Oh, I'm tellin' Nanny.

KIM  You said a bad word.

STEPHEN  Bold, Granda.

PATRICK  Okay, okay. I'll chase you. Just don't tell your Nanny what I said.

ESTHER  And he was happy. He had his pension, we owned the house and life was good. And in 1992. There was a knock on the door.

PATRICK  Who is it?

ESTHER  It's the post man.

PATRICK  The kids are runnin' me ragged, I'm bollocksed.

ESTHER  It was a letter. For Patrick. He opened it and his face dropped.

PATRICK  Jesus Christ.

ESTHER  What is it?

PATRICK  It's from her.

ESTHER  What?

PATRICK  A letter, from Anne Brady.

*We see* ANNE *and she steps forward.*

ANNE  My dear Patrick,

I've written this letter at least fifty times since I left you and thrown out each and every one. I've thought about calling you, writing you and seeing you my entire life. When I was twenty-two years old I had you in a house on Railway Street. I was a prostitute. I had nothing, absolutely nothing, just you. I knew deep in my soul that if I kept you, you would've died in my arms as we slept in a doorway somewhere, so I did what I thought was best. I left you with a kind and loving family in the hope that they would do what I couldn't, give you love, life and safety. I just want you to know that I love you and always will. I have not long left in this world, a few weeks, I'm told by the doctors, so I guess I just wanted you to know that giving you up is the hardest thing I've ever had to do. I have given you nothing in this world so I would now like to leave you with this. This is a brooch of May Oblong's, she was the madam that I worked for all those years ago. I have been told that it's worth a substantial amount of money so I would like you to have it. Please forgive me, I did what I felt was best.

Love always, Anne.

**ANNE** *steps back into the shadows.*

**ESTHER**  And she died a few days after we received that letter. She died alone, in Galway, with nothing to her name but a brooch. Now Patrick's. Which he had priced.

**PATRICK**  What? How fuckin' much?

**ESTHER**  Language!

**PATRICK**  Did you hear that, Esther?

**ESTHER**  He exaggerated a little but it was worth a nice bit of money.

**PATRICK**  I want to open savings accounts for my three grandchildren.

**ESTHER**  And that's what he did with it and we didn't touch a cent of it, he left all to the children and Francis. We both travelled, saw the world. A million miles from the world we grew up in. And...and as the years went on he started to lose his mind. First little things/

**PATRICK**  Esther, where are me keys?

**ESTHER**  But they got worse.

PATRICK  Where am I?

ESTHER  And worse.

PATRICK  Who are you?

ESTHER  He was diagnosed with Alzheimer's in 2011. I couldn't look after him. So he went to the Meath Community Unit in 2013. And I went every day. And by then he didn't remember me or the kids...he just remembered the fuckin' docks. God forgive me for cursin'. It's all he'd talk to the nurses about.

PATRICK  There was this thing called the read, and if your name was called you worked, if it wasn't, you didn't.

ESTHER  He was happy.

PATRICK  Me da, Paulie, brought me down.

ESTHER  Livin' in his stories.

PATRICK  I was Little Paulie.

ESTHER  Content in them.

PATRICK  He brought me on to the coal boats.

ESTHER  He was happiest down the docks.

PATRICK  I'd to piss on me hands.

ESTHER  I think all the men were.

PATRICK  Back-breaking work.

ESTHER  The community/

PATRICK  But down in the hatch/

ESTHER  The freedom/

PATRICK  With the boys.

ESTHER  It was a family.

PATRICK  I miss those days.

ESTHER  And one day he came back to me.

PATRICK  Esther?

**ESTHER**  For just a moment.

**PATRICK**  Esther?

**ESTHER**  Yes, love.

*Pause.*

**PATRICK**  Sorry I stood on your feet.

**ESTHER**  It's okay, love. You got better.

**PATRICK**  I did, didn't I?

**ESTHER**  You did. You were the best.

**PATRICK**  You were the best.

*Pause.*

Right, I've to get back to the docks.

*Pause.*

**ESTHER**  You do. Go back to the docks, my love.

*Music plays and the dialogue is spoken again but slower and the weight of each word felt, as if a lament. This can be repeated, depending on the director's preference.*

**VOICE**  Down the docks.

**VOICE**  Up the Monto.

**VOICE**  In the Tenements.

**VOICE**  The rot of Dublin.

**VOICE**  Rats in your bed.

**VOICE**  Flies in the walls.

**VOICE**  The unfortunate girls.

**VOICE**  The unfortunate boys.

**VOICE**  The unfortunate families.

**VOICE**  No work today.

**VOICE**   No food today.

**VOICE**   No hope today.

**VOICE**   The worst slums in Europe.

**VOICE**   Collapsing on us.

**VOICE**   Killing us.

**VOICE**   That's where Dublin came from.

**VOICES**   Out of the shit.

**VOICES**   And into the world.

### The End

# VISIT THE SAMUEL FRENCH BOOKSHOP AT THE ROYAL COURT THEATRE

## Browse plays and theatre books, get expert advice and enjoy a coffee

Samuel French Bookshop
Royal Court Theatre
Sloane Square
London
SW1W 8AS
020 7565 5024

## Shop from thousands of titles on our website

 **samuelfrench.co.uk**

 **samuelfrenchltd**

 **samuel french uk**

Lightning Source UK Ltd.
Milton Keynes UK
UKHW021824290319
340172UK00002B/9/P